AN ARTIST?

God Has Six Gifts For You

AN ARTIST?: *God Has Six Gifts For You*
By Alma Villegas, PhD
ISBN: 9798639354311
Imprint: Independently published

Cover art and design: Alma Villegas
Inside book layout: Alma Villegas
Photo of Alma Villegas on back cover: Zahira Villegas-González
Translation by: Betty Austin Muñoz, Zahira Villegas-González and Alma Villegas

The Gift of Art
New York & Puerto Rico, 2020
www.AlmaVillegas.net

AN ARTIST?

God Has Six Gifts For You

Alma Villegas

Based on
Bezalel, an Artist Called by God

Towards a Theology of Art Collection
Bezalel Series, Volume 1B

THE GIFT OF ART
Connecting Heaven and Earth Through the Arts

for glory and for beauty
Exodus 28:2

New York & Puerto Rico, 2020

DEDICATION

To

Moisés Villegas Fernandez, Jr.

My beloved brother, who,
every time I have confronted a
mountain that seems to scream at me,
"Alma, this is as far as you go,"
has been by my side, telling me,
"Go forward. With Christ, you can do it."

To

Daniel Montañez

I saw how he created and directed
the first theatrical performances in the
church and created and directed the
Grupo de AVIVAMIENTO.

To

Grupo de AVIVAMIENTO

Especially to the members during the
first thirteen years of the group (1967–1980),
with whom I grew up physically and spiritually and with
whom I shared my first artistic dreams of moving on to
change the world.

Also, to all the members who have followed.

NOTE TO THE READER

As a way to reach more readers with the message of the Theology of Art and to please those who want to read small books, we have divided *Bezalel, an Artist Called by God* in three parts. They were divided taking into account the main themes of the book. The Introduction, Conclusion and Appendices remain the same across the three books. They are:

- *GOD CHOSE AN ARTIST*
  Bezalel's Call, Volume 1A
- *AN ARTIST?*
  God Has Six Gifts for You, Volume 1B
- *OBEDIENCE AND SUBMISSION,*
  The Key to Bezalel's Success, Volume 1C

SEE, I HAVE CALLED

Now the Lord spoke to Moses, saying:

See, I have called by name Bezalel the son of Uri, the son of Hur, of the tribe of Judah. I have filled him with the Spirit of God in wisdom, in understanding, in knowledge, and in all manner of craftsmanship to devise artistic works for work with gold, with silver, and with bronze, and in the cutting of stones for settings, and in carving of wood, to work in all manner of craftsmanship.

Exodus 31:1–5

Moses said to the children of Israel:

See, the Lord has called by name Bezalel the son of Uri, the son of Hur, of the tribe of Judah. And He has filled him with the Spirit of God, in wisdom, in understanding, and in knowledge, and in all manner of craftsmanship, to design artistic works, to work in gold, in silver, and in bronze, and in the cutting of stones for settings and in the carving of wood in order to make every manner of artistic work.

He also has put in his heart to teach, both he and Oholiab, the son of Ahisamak, of the tribe of Dan. He has filled them with skill to do all manner of work as craftsmen; as designers; as embroiderers in blue, in purple, in scarlet, and in fine linen; and as weavers: as craftsmen of every work and artistic designers.

Exodus 35:30–35

CONTENTS

INTRODUCTION
TO THE WISE HARTED..1
   THE SPIRIT OF GOD...3
   WISDOM..15
   UNDERSTANDING...37
   KNOWLEDGE 47
   ART..57
   ABILITY TO TEACH 77
CONCLUSION 85
   TOWARDS A THEOLOGY OF ART 87
APPENDICES 91
   APPENDIX A: ART IN THE PROPHETIC PLAN......................93
   APPENDIX B: LIZETTE AYALA LETTER (1980) 109
   APPENDIX C: OPENING NEW PATHWAYS 111
   BIBLIOGRAPHY...113
   ABOUT THE AUTHOR..115

INTRODUCTION
LORD, MAKE ME A WOMAN OF IDEAS

IN SEARCH OF A DREAM

In June of 1980, I left Puerto Rico for England and New York in pursuit of a beautiful dream: to do graduate studies in theater, with the purpose of using it as a transforming agent and so that people could see through it the reflection of a Creator God. There was in me an immense thirst for artistic knowledge that could enable me to accomplish my goals. I'd already had the experience of working with a group of young people and seeing what God could do when we put our talents and skills in their hands. However, reaching that moment of decision in my life was not an easy path. First, discovering and accepting my artistic talents meant going against what, at that time, was accepted by the Church in general, and second, daring to take the step and start moving in a way that I suspected was the will of God required all my faith and courage. Many times, people said to me:

--- "Christ is coming, and you are going to study...WHAT? THEATER?"

--- "Oh...so you want to be an 'actress'?"

--- "Are you telling me that God had called you to serve Him through the arts? Are you sure?"
--- "Are you telling me that art is a gift from God?"

--- "The Lord told me that you can't rehearse the play in the church."

These questions and statements came from pastors, presidents of evangelical denominations, Christian leaders, and so forth. I was so intimidated. And with each pronouncement, my insecurities grew. I had many questions and fears: "Am I doing something against the will of God?" "Am I doing something dishonest?" "Am I going to lose my salvation? "Am I going to hell?" "Am I becoming mundane?" I was so confused.

MY BEGINNINGS

I accepted Jesus as my Savior at 16 and started attending youth meetings. But one night, as I arrived at a youth meeting, I found out that we would have a planning session to come up with ideas and activities for the upcoming Youth Week, and I found myself unable to present any ideas. I was making such a big effort to comply with what I understood, at that time, was to serve God that I had put Him in a religious box, and as a consequence, creative ideas were not flowing because I was afraid of them. That night, I prayed to God. Right where I was sitting, I turned my face to the white wall I was leaning against, and I just told Him, "Lord, make me a woman of ideas." I was surprised to hear myself saying such a prayer, so much so that I still remember not only the moment, but the exact words pronounced. I understood that it was an inward cry coming from the bottom of my being, although I could not understand how or why those words had come from my mouth.

Until that moment, I had never had a goal for my life. I knew that I wanted to study because my parents continually repeated the importance of an education, but study what? I was only excited about music, dance, painting, and poetry, but that was something that was very far from my reality, so I discarded them from my life. Therefore, I had not stopped to think about what I was going to study, and I do not remember other dreams or future ambitions.

Additionally, I discovered that if I wanted to consecrate my life to the Lord Jesus, I could not participate in anything artistic. For example, cinema, theater, and dance or acting classes, among other artistic endeavors, were not accepted in the Church. I understood that my love for Jesus was greater than my love for the arts, so it was no problem becoming a science teacher.

I now recognize that one of the first things that Jesus did after saving my life was awaken my dreams. Those dreams had been forgotten, and I had no idea they were still inside of me. Those dreams were not dead, but dormant, asleep. Before the presence of the Creator God, my dreams were awakened. And the Spirit of God, who searches everything, even the most intimate parts of our heart, made me exclaim, "Lord, make me a woman of ideas." I understand that God heard that prayer. I believe it was a prayer that came out of the heart of God, and it became a seed inside my spirit. There are moments when we believe that we are the ones praying, but then we realize that it is the Spirit of God placing the prayer into our spirit. The Spirit of God was moving over my spirit to incubate, to nurture, the calling that God put in me before the foundation of the world.

To my surprise, the answer to this prayer manifested itself through art, especially theater. Artistic ideas emerged again. I created several theater groups, wrote some plays and after several theater production, I decided to study theater, dance and visual arts. But I became even more confused. Where do ideas come from? I was seeking the Lord with all my heart, so why did I have this strong inclination towards the arts, towards the theater. The fear of turning away from God arose once again. But this time, I asked God. Only He could have the correct answer.

MY ENCOUNTER WITH BEZALEL

This was an experience that impacted my life drastically. When I felt the direct opposition that most of the churches were displaying in relation to art, a question arose from within me: "What does the Bible say about art?" I had learned that the Bible is above any revelation or prophetic word. So, with great *naïveté* on my part, I asked God where, in the Bible, the passages concerning art were. And I say *naïveté* because it seems strange to me now that it never occurred to me to consult a concordance, Bible dictionary, or encyclopedia, much less ask the pastor. I thought mine was a question that only God could answer, and for the next three months, I sat in a pew in the prayer room in my church with the Bible on my lap, repeating the same prayer over and over, "Lord, show me where in your Word does it say that art comes from you."

What I discovered in the Bible changed my relationship with God and my destiny forever. One evening, my Bible fell to the floor, and when I picked it up, my eyes looked at Exodus 31:3: "And I have filled him with the spirit of God, in wisdom, and in understanding, and in knowledge, and in all manner of workmanship." But in the Spanish version, instead of workmanship, it says, "ART." WOW and WOW. The answer that I was looking for was in front of my eyes. The arts may be forbidden in many churches, but not in God's WORD. What an amazing revelation! What an amazing God!

A year after that experience, I found myself on an airplane on my way to England to study theater. And to clarify, no, my destiny didn't change; the Bible just pointed to my real destiny, and I became the theater director, playwright, and theology of art scholar that God ordained and sanctified me to be even before He formed me in the womb. And this, my dear sister and brother, is why I wanted to write this book: I have a story to tell you about that dream to become an artist. In the early days, becoming an artist brought many challenges to my life as one sector of the church did not understand the potential of art as an instrument of worship, evangelism, and emotional, physical, and spiritual healing, among other things. But I already had discovered in the Bible, through Bezalel, the *Poiesis Theou*…the Creator God, inexhaustible source of inspiration and artistic revelation.

God makes no distinction of person. He longs to reach all mankind. There are those who are sensitive to the beauty of a flower, and there are those who are excited to see a basketball game, read a philosophy book, or be a Brazilian jiu-jitsu black belt. And as the Creator God, He understands that some will be touched through the testimony of a boxer like Manny Pacquiao or the preaching by a pastor or an evangelist. But He knows better than anyone, because He made us, that there are others who will need theater, music, dance, cinema, visual arts—in short, the creative arts—to be touched and transformed by the power of God. I remember that once God whispered in my spirit, "As an artist, you will be able to reach places that others cannot because, usually, artists tend to be welcome everywhere," and so it has been. I feel grateful to God because I understand that he gave me the gift of art as an instrument to transform and literally save lives.

Art is a gift from God. I want you to discover and study the life of Bezalel, an artist called and supernaturally gifted by God. Here, you will find Bezalel's call, his divine mandate, his spiritual and artistic training, and the personal characteristics that made him, along with his work team, wise artists at heart. In the same way, God is calling you to transform your natural talents into supernatural so that you become like Bezalel, a wise artist at heart.

The Bible tells us in Ephesians 3:20–21, "Now to Him who is able to do exceedingly abundantly beyond all that we ask or imagine, according to the power that works in us, to Him be the glory in the church and in Christ Jesus throughout all generations, forever and ever. Amen." And I am a witness to this creative and artistic abundance of God.

TO THE WISE-HEARTED

CHAPTER 1

THE SPIRIT OF GOD
Creative Inspiration

> I have filled him with the Spirit of God.
> (Exodus 31:3)

DIVINE PREPARATION

Concerning Bezalel, there are some verses that we have not analyzed and that, along with Exodus 31:2, are the cornerstone of his calling. I am referring to Exodus 31:3, "I have filled him with the Spirit of God in wisdom, in understanding, in knowledge, and in all manner of craftsmanship," and Exodus 35:34a, "He also has put in his heart to teach…" These two verses speak about the preparation of Bezalel to be able to do the work. Let us examine the verse within the context that we have already studied. When God speaks to Moses at Mount Sinai, He says:

> Now the Lord spoke to Moses, saying: See, I have called by name Bezalel the son of Uri, the son of Hur, of the tribe of Judah. **I have filled him with the Spirit of God in wisdom,**

in understanding, in knowledge, and in all manner of craftsmanship to devise artistic works for work with gold, with silver, and with bronze, and in the cutting of stones for settings, and in carving of wood, to work in all manner of craftsmanship. (Exodus 31:1–5, emphasis added)

While Moses speaks with the people of Israel to notify them of what the Lord said, He tells them, "He also has put in his heart to teach…" (Exodus 35:34 a).

God tells Moses that Bezalel has been called and been separated for the construction of the Tabernacle, and He immediately tells him that Bezalel has been filled with the Spirit of God to achieve the goal. In addition to this, the Lord grants Bezalel other gifts: wisdom, understanding, knowledge, artistic skill, and teaching ability, which, together with the Spirit of God, make six gifts in total.

To be able to read about Bezalel's calling and, in particular, how Moses shared Bezalel's calling with the people of Israel, is, to me, one of the special moments of Bezalel's story. I understand that these verses hold the spiritual key that can open a creative treasure for all of us artists of the 21st century, and if one appropriates them, one can change the outcome of Christian and secular art. To me, these verses establish the biblical foundation of what I consider a theology of art to be. It is for this reason that I am going to dedicate the next chapters to exploring the supernatural qualifications given by God to Bezalel that made him eligible to not only do the work but also direct the construction of the Tabernacle.

Just for mere curiosity, I took it upon myself to search for the meaning of the word "filled" in Hebrew and found that it is *malĕ¹*. *Malĕ* is a verb that means "filled, plenty, complete, to fill the hand and consecrate." In other words, God gave plenty of His Spirit to Bezalel. We are talking about abundance, totality. It seems wonderful that the word also means to "fill the hands," which could immediately be associated with anointing. One can see in Mark 16:18 that Jesus says, "They will lay hands on the sick, and they will recover." The hands represent the ability to do work and solve problems. They also represent responsibility, and for the artist, especially an architect or a visual artist, the hands are their main work instrument. When the Lord gave instructions

4

concerning the garments for the priests to Moses, He said, "You shall put them on Aaron your brother, and on his sons with him, and shall anoint them, and consecrate them, and sanctify them, that they may minister to Me as priests" (Exodus 28:41). Bezalel was filled with God's Spirit. He was dedicated, sanctified, and separated for the work that he was about to do. His hands were filled with the necessary gifts for the work and anointed for the labor, and the responsibility of the project was invested and awarded to Bezalel. What a beautiful way to start the building of the Tabernacle, accepting the calling of "Let them make Me a sanctuary that I may dwell among them" (Exodus 25:8).

THE SPIRIT OF GOD

Let us remember that the first thing God says to Moses about Bezalel is that he has been filled with the Spirit of God. Then Moses summons the people of Israel, and he repeats the same words that God told him.

Bezalel is the first person in the Scriptures where God Himself gives witness that he is filled with the Spirit. It is one of the first quotes in the Bible about the Spirit of God and the first where it is indicated that God has filled a person with His Spirit for a specific task. If we make reference to what is known in biblical hermeneutics as the law of the first mention, we must recognize that these words from God to Moses have great significance and establish an important precedent.

First of all, to know that the first person of whom God Himself gives testimony, saying that he has been filled with the Spirit of God, is an artist is of great excitement to me. The whole creative essence within yourself is awakened, you enter into a state of alert, and your spirit stands up, saying, "WOW! This is for me!" However, I continue to ask myself, how is it that no one told me that Bezalel was an artist? How is it that no one told me what God Himself told Moses? God told Moses, the prophet, the priest, the leader, the deliverer, with whom He spent 40 days and 40 nights to give him the Ten Commandments and all the laws, "See, I have called Bezalel…and I have filled him with the Spirit of God." Oh, how wonderful! Again, I emphasize, when God mentions something for the first time in His Word, it needs to be paid attention. And I ask myself, what is God saying to me as an artist?

Throughout the Holy Scriptures, we see how being filled with the Spirit of God becomes the main requirement to be called by God. And if it is taken into consideration that this is the first declaration given to an artist, it is of great transcendence to me. First, God speaks to Moses and tells him, "I have filled him with the Spirit of God…" (Exodus 31:3b), and then Moses repeats these words to the people when he summons them, "all the congregation of the children of Israel together" (Exodus 35:1), and he tells them, "See, the Lord has called by name Bezalel… And He has filled him with the Spirit of God" (Exodus 35:30, 31a).

We all know that in the Old Testament, the Spirit of God was available to the prophet, the priest, and the king. Nevertheless, the first mention that God makes about the filling of the Spirit of God and its importance to be equipped for the work to be done happens when He calls and separates Bezalel, the artist, to do the work of constructing the Tabernacle. Bezalel was not a prophet, a priest, nor a king! *Ruwach*[2] is the Hebrew word for spirit, for breath, and *Elohiym*[3] is the Supreme God. Thus, God filled Bezalel with His own breath, with the Spirit of the Almighty.

Another important observation that I have is the context in which the process of the calling of Bezalel occurs. The circumstances surrounding the revelation from God to Moses about who would be building the Tabernacle were the same as when God gave him the tables of the law and the description of the Tabernacle. Therefore, if the previous details were important, so was this last one. God would not speak about such transcendental subjects like the law, day of rest, and the Tabernacle only to then change and speak about something insignificant. The person and his assistants who would build the Tabernacle were highly important to the Lord, so much so that we know their names and the names of their parents, families, and the tribes where they belonged, and they all had significant names, as we have previously noticed. So I, as an artist, have to understand that I have a special value before God and that the first gift that He gives me is His Spirit.

6

Sometimes I wonder why, after God told Moses that Bezalel has been filled with the Spirit of God, Moses went before the people with all the instructions that God gave to communicate to them, and he also announced the calling of Bezalel. I imagine the surprise of many when they realized that God had called an artist and that the first thing He did was fill him with the Spirit. Would it be to eliminate any doubt among the people that the work to be done was sacred? I am sure that the people had seen artistic expressions in Egypt, and it was with all assurance that they had seen them in the context of idolatry. Before the imminent construction of a sanctuary to the Lord, a distinction as to requirements and skills was established for all who received the assignment of constructing the Tabernacle. Maybe it was necessary so that there would be no doubt in the people today that God calls artists and fills them with His Spirit to construct the church of the 21st century. Even now, the names of Bezalel and Oholiab have been preserved as a sign of what God can do when we, as artists, answer the calling of God. Moses, as the leader, received confirmation about Bezalel's calling, and he told it to the people. God separated them for this work; that way, there would be no room for doubts and jealousy. God chose them for the work, and His Spirit prepared them.

It was the first time that a sanctuary was designed and built for worship and service unto God. It would consist of artistic elements, but above all, the structure of the Tabernacle, with all its different areas of service and worship, every piece of furniture, and every accessory, foreshadowed He who was to come. Nowadays, when we study the Tabernacle, we see that it is a prototype of Christ and His redeeming work, and that message came to us free from alterations and/or modifications. A Tabernacle designed in the mind of God needed obedient artists filled with the Spirit of God to be able to recognize and follow obediently the instructions given. God speaks to our spirit through His Spirit: "But God has revealed them to us by His Spirit. For the Spirit searches all things, yes, the deep things of God" (1 Corinthians 2:10). Thus, the Spirit needed to move upon Bezalel. I understand that no matter how brilliant or talented Bezalel and those who collaborated with him in the construction of the Tabernacle were, there was no way they would have done the work according to their own effort. They needed a divine mind like the mind of God and an instrument subject to obedience like Bezalel.

Once again, I want to emphasize the order and spiritual protocol to which we, as artists, must be subject to. Bezalel was identified by his family and tribe, something like being a member of a congregation, and when the time of the calling comes, God speaks and confirms that calling through the spiritual leader. And Moses notified the congregation. I am almost sure that way before this declaration of God unto Moses, God was preparing Bezalel. But at the moment of making it public, God confirmed the calling through Moses, his spiritual leader.

It would be wonderful for many of us if, at the moment of our initiation into the arts ministry, the pastor notified and confirmed the artistic calling of God in our lives to the congregation. Instead, many feel rejected and disoriented because of the lack of recognition of art as a gift from God by many of our leaders. Many young people and adults, and I mention adults because art is not only for children and youths, feel frustrated because they cannot develop their artistic gifts in a healthy and successful way.

THE SPIRIT OF GOD AND CREATIVITY

While learning about the Spirit of God, I saw in Genesis 1:2, where it says, "And the earth was without form and void, and the darkness was upon the face of the deep, and the Spirit of God moved upon the face of the waters." Why was the Spirit moving upon the waters? Seeking clarification, I searched in the Biblia Peshitta (Spanish version, 2006), which is the translation of the Word of God in Aramaic, one of the oldest manuscripts of the Bible, and it says, "Y el Espíritu de Dios incubaba sobre la superficie de las aguas",[4] which is to say "And the Spirit of God incubated upon the face of the waters" instead of "moved upon the face of the waters."

Remember, the word "incubated," instead of "moved or moving," brings forth a much broader view of the Spirit of God in the creative process. To incubate is to develop the necessary conditions to create life. Birds lie on top of their eggs to incubate

8

them. This maintains a temperature of constant heat so that the embryo inside can grow. Incubation speaks to providing the necessary conditions to create life. The Spirit of God was creating the necessary conditions so that the matter that was going to be created from ex-nihilo (made from nothing) would respond to the voice of God and would take form. The Bible immediately tells us, "God said, 'Let there be light,' and there was light" (Genesis 1:3).

The word in Hebrew for Spirit is *rŭwach*, which is also described as the breath-wind-spirit of God. Therefore, the breath-wind-spirit of God was moving, incubating upon the face of the waters like an eagle fanning his eggs. The eagle fans his wings over his eggs to take care of them, protect them. Such is the way that we see the Spirit of God as an integral part of creation. The Psalmist confirms this creative work of the Spirit of God when he says, "When You send forth Your Spirit, they are created, and You renew the surface of the ground" (Psalm 104:30).

In the same manner, the Spirit would dwell upon Bezalel, incubating ideas, nurturing his creating capabilities for the work he would have to do. The Tabernacle had to be built according to the divine design by people whom the Holy Spirit would incubate the gifts and talents given to them to be developed positively. The work to be done was described to Moses by God, and there is a possibility that very little space was given for changes or creative variations. Truly, Bezalel needed the Spirit of God to face the task.

Since we have been created in the image and likeness of God, we have creative capabilities within us, but God creates from nothing, and we create with the matter that has already been created. And that is because God, as Creator/Father, shares His creative nature with human beings. That is why it should not be strange to see the Spirit of God upon Bezalel; God knew that Bezalel possessed the necessary elements to be incubated, nurtured, and developed.

THE SPIRIT OF GOD AND EXCELLENCE

Besides identifying the Spirit of God with the creating process, He also outstands Himself by the excellence of His work.

9

The excellence and integrity in the way a work is done allows you to distinguish yourself from people who do not know God. Such was the experience between Joseph and Pharaoh: "Pharaoh said to his servants, 'Can we find anyone like this man, in whom is the Spirit of God?'" (Genesis 41:38). To Pharaoh, Joseph was able to do the work that others could not do, and he could do it well. He surpassed all expectations, and that is excellence. This is the first time we see the Bible tell us that the Spirit of God is with a person. This time, the testimony does not come straight from God, like it did with Bezalel. It comes from Pharaoh, which is very interesting considering that Pharaoh did not know God, but Joseph, by interpreting Pharaoh's dreams, was able to manifest the Spirit of God, and Pharaoh, although he did not fear God nor serve Him, was able to see God in Joseph. It is also interesting to note that Joseph extended his talents unto the service of Pharaoh, to the service of a secular deed but honoring God through the process, and God was glorified. This is the beginning of the tearing down of imposed schemes: making Christian art that honors God can only be done within the Church.

THE SPIRIT OF GOD AND THE MINISTRY OF JESUS

We know that the Holy Spirit is crucial in our development and preparation, so much so that the same Jesus needed the Spirit to help with His ministry. We know that Jesus is the Son of God, but the Bible tells us that He became man and dwelled among us. Thus, as a man, He needed the Spirit of God.

In the Old Testament, the prophet Isaiah tells us how God trained him: "And there shall come forth a shoot from the stump of Jesse, and a Branch shall grow out of his roots. The Spirit of the Lord shall rest upon him" (Isaiah 11:1, 2a). The prophet announces his origin or his roots, his birth, and his capability. We see here the reference of how the Holy Spirit will be upon him. Jesus will be anointed for His ministry, which happens while He is being baptized by John the Baptist: "Now when all the people were baptized, and when Jesus also had been baptized and was praying, the heavens were opened, and the Holy Spirit descended in a bodily form like a dove on Him, and a voice came from heaven which said, 'You are My beloved Son. In You I am well pleased' (Luke 3:21–22). The Apostle Luke continues: "Jesus, being filled with the Holy Spirit, returned from the Jordan and was led by the Spirit into the wilderness" (Luke 4:1). When Jesus went into the wilderness after establishing His ministry, He was full of the Spirit. How many of us go out into the ministry without an idea of what is the anointing and how it can help us, "When the devil had ended all the temptations, he departed from Him until another time" (Luke 4:13). The testimony of Apostle Luke continues to emphasize how the role of the Spirit was essential in Jesus' ministry:

The scroll of the prophet Isaiah was handed to Him.

When He had unrolled the scroll,

He found the place where it was written:

"The Spirit of the Lord is upon Me,
  because He has anointed Me
  to preach the gospel to the poor;
He has sent Me to heal the broken-hearted,
  to preach deliverance to the captives
  and recovery of sight to the blind,
to set at liberty those who are oppressed;
  to preach the acceptable year of the Lord."

Then He rolled up the scroll, and He gave it back to the attendant, and sat down. The eyes of all those who were in the synagogue were fixed on Him. And He began to say to them, "Today this Scripture is fulfilled in your hearing." (Luke 4:17–21)

Jesus started His ministry full of the Spirit. The Spirit transformed Him from a natural man into a man whom all wondered about the way He expressed Himself: "All bore witness to Him, and wondered at the gracious words which came from His mouth. Then they said, 'Is this not Joseph's son?'" (Luke 4:22). He was still a man, but no longer a natural man; he was a spiritual man. He had been anointed by the Holy Spirit: "How God anointed Jesus of Nazareth with the Holy Spirit and with power, who went about doing good and healing all who were oppressed by the devil, for God was with Him" (Acts 10:38).

This privilege of being filled with the Holy Spirit would not continue to be just for the priests, prophets, and kings. Jesus Himself gave us the promise of the Holy Spirit to all: "I will pray to the Father, and He will give you another Counselor, that He may be with you forever: the Spirit of truth, whom the world cannot receive, for it does not see Him, neither does it know Him. But you know Him, for He lives with you, and will be in you" (John 14:16–17).

After His death and resurrection, Jesus tells His disciples and the followers to not leave from Jerusalem but to wait for the promise of the Father: "For John baptized with water, but you shall be baptized with the Holy Spirit not many days from now" (Acts 1:5). And He explained the importance of receiving the promise: "But you shall receive power when the Holy Spirit comes upon you. And you shall be My witnesses in Jerusalem, and in all Judea and Samaria, and to the ends of the earth" (Acts 1:8). And one sees how, on the day of Pentecost, they were all filled with the Holy Ghost.

What a blessing. Being filled with the Spirit of God to carry on with our calling seems to be easier today than what it was back in the days of Bezalel. The Spirit of God enriched the natural capabilities in Bezalel and transformed them into extraordinary ones. This is the first lesson that we learn and the first gift we receive towards the implementation of the theology of art within our artistic calling.

NOTES

[1] James Strong, LL.D., S.T.D., *The New Strong's Expanded Exhaustive Concordance of the Bible,* (Nashville: Thomas Nelson, 2010), 158.

[2] _____, *The New Strong's Expanded Exhaustive Concordance of the Bible,* (Nashville: Thomas Nelson, 2010), 258–259.

[3] _____, *The New Strong's Expanded Exhaustive Concordance of the Bible*, (Nashville: Thomas Nelson, 2010), 17.

[4] Instituto Cultural Álef y Tau, A.C., *La Biblia Peshita en Español*, (Nashville: Broadman & Holdman Publishing Group, 2006), 1.

CHAPTER 2

WISDOM
Creative Process

> And I have filled him of the Spirit of God in wisdom...
> (Exodus 31:3b)

ABILITY TO CREATE SUPERNATURALLY

Since the beginning of creation, God has done things much more abundantly than "we ask or imagine," as Ephesians 3:20 tells us. And we see this manifested in the call of Bezalel. Not only does God call him by his name and point out that He has filled him with His Spirit, but he also continues to declare the gifts He has placed in him. The call or separation for the task has not been enough; being full of the Spirit has been a wonderful thing, but it is not the end of training, but the beginning that opens the door for other gifts. We serve a God of superabundance. So, immediately after God told Moses that Bezalel had been filled with the Spirit of God, He tells him that He has given him wisdom (Exodus 31:3b). This is also confirmed before the congregation (Exodus 35:1).

The word "wisdom" comes to us from the Hebrew *chokmah*.[1]

It appears for the first time in Exodus 28:3, in context with the artistic activity. I checked four Bible translations:

> And thou shalt speak unto all that are **wise hearted, whom I have filled with the spirit of wisdom**, that they may make Aaron's garments to consecrate him, that he may minister unto me in the priest's office. (KJV)

> "So you shall speak to all *who are* gifted artisans, **whom I have filled with the spirit of wisdom**, that they may make Aaron's garments, to consecrate him, that he may minister to Me as priest (NKJV).

> You shall speak to all who are specially skilled, **whom I have filled with the spirit of wisdom**, that they may make Aaron's garments to consecrate him, that he may minister to Me as a priest. (MEV)

> Call all the **skilled workers** to whom I have given **ability**, and tell them to make Aaron's clothes, so that he may be dedicated as a priest in my service. (GNT)

When describing the men and women who were going to participate in the making of the garments, the Lord describes them as wise-hearted, gifted artisans, specially gifted and skilled workers. That description comes from the Hebrew word *chakam*,[2] which means wise, wise-hearted, intelligent, skillful, or artful. These were people God had filled with the spirit of wisdom, or to whom He had given ability. The Hebrew word for "wisdom," "ability," "skillful" is *chokmah*. The word "wisdom" is associated, in this verse, with the technical knowledge or special skills needed to make the garments. And we have seen that, when God calls Bezalel, He says that he has given him wisdom (chokmah). Two things we can infer here: that the special abilities that the artist had were given by God, or his natural abilities as an artist were transformed into supernatural abilities. No matter which of the two options is your case, the important thing is that, like Bezalel, you will always end up with God's supernatural touch in your artistic life.

In Bezalel's case, it was artistic wisdom, artistic ability, or the capacity to do things. I really prefer to use the word "wisdom" because it has a stronger connotation, even though one of the definitions of wisdom is ability. Wisdom is one of those words difficult to define in a single sentence. For some, wisdom is the ability to make the right decisions, which is a sign of maturity. According to Strong, a person with *chokmah* could be a warrior or an artist, depending on the vocation that's been followed. *Chokmah* is also that thought or first revelation of understanding that we receive as we are in the process of learning a new subject or a new lesson. It is like an intuition or a perspective of being able to see the whole plan in its totality, to see how everything falls into place, receiving the whole picture of what the project will be. According to *Psychology Today*, "wisdom" derives from the Proto-Indo-European root *weid-*, "to see."[3] I love that. Can you imagine? When you, as an artist, are filled with the spirit of wisdom, "you can see" beyond the natural into the supernatural realm and get artistic ideas, concepts, and designs literarily out of this world.

In Isaiah 11:2, the spirit of wisdom is one of the seven spirits the prophet said would rest upon the renewal of Jesse, the promised Messiah, Jesus of Nazareth. The word wisdom, to me as a theater director, playwright, and author, is very valuable. If, for Bezalel to be able to do the work for which He was called, he was filled with the spirit of wisdom, then I understand that it is necessary for me as an artist to have it. If even Jesus, being the Son of God, had to be infilled with wisdom to be able to develop His ministry here on earth, then, for me, it is transcendental.

I have asked myself how this wisdom given to Bezalel by the Spirit of God could also be relevant to my artistic career. In the book of Proverbs, we hear wisdom speaking, and we see how it can guide us when we turn to it: "Turn at my reproof; surely I will pour out my spirit on you; I will make my words known to you" (Proverbs 1:23). Therefore, in this historic moment when art is beginning to come forth in a significant way within the Church and the Christian communities, we need to be led by wisdom; we need to hear from it.

WISDOM AND THE CREATIVE PROCESS WITHIN CREATION

We have seen how the Spirit of God moved at the beginning of creation, incubating within the face of the waters. In the same way, wisdom was part of that creative process, "The Lord by wisdom has founded the earth" (Proverbs 3:19). It is an inherent part of God: "The Lord possessed me in the beginning of His way, before His works of old" (Proverbs 8:22). And it was present before the heavens and earth were created, even before the foundation of the world:

> I was set up from everlasting,
>   from the beginning, before there was ever an earth.
> When there were no depths, I was brought forth,
>   when there were no fountains abounding with water.
> Before the mountains were settled,
>   before the hills I was brought forth;
> while as yet He had not made the earth or the fields,
>   or the first dust of the world. (Proverbs 8:23–26)

We can see wisdom as creative energy or as part of creation since it was an intricate part of the whole creative process of the universe:

> When He prepared the heavens, I was there,
>   when He drew a circle on the face of the deep,
> when He established the clouds above,
>   when He strengthened the fountains of the deep,
>
> when He gave to the sea His decree,
>   that the waters should not pass His commandment,
> when He appointed the foundations of the earth. (Proverbs 8:27–29)

Even after the creation was completed, wisdom remained present:

> Then I was by Him, as one brought up with Him;
> and I was daily His delight,
>   rejoicing always before Him,
> rejoicing in the habitable part of His earth,
>   and my delights were with the sons of men. (Proverbs

8:30–31).

How wonderful! If wisdom was present throughout the whole process of the creation of such a majestic universe, could that same wisdom assist us in creating artistic works? Art as a reflection of our God? Can wisdom help us create new theatrical works that do not have to be adapted from work written by those who do not fear God? Would wisdom be able to help us create new acting techniques? New cinematography techniques? New theatrical techniques? New styles of acting, design, or even stage direction? New musical rhythms? New artistic theory that can identify with our Christian faith? I am sure that the answer to all of these is a definite YES!

JOSEPH, SOLOMON, AND DANIEL

Joseph, Solomon, and Daniel are three examples of the wisdom of God. Let us examine what kind of impact they had, not only on the personal level but how they impacted events nationally and internationally as well. Pharaoh recognized God through the wisdom that Joseph received from God:

> Pharaoh said to his servants, "Can we find anyone like this man, in whom is the Spirit of God?"

> And Pharaoh said to Joseph, "Since God has shown you all this, there is no one as discerning and wise as you. (Genesis 41:38–39).

And Joseph was placed in a position of authority to lead a unique mission. Pharaoh delegates to Joseph the highest authority position right after his own. He gave Joseph his ring, clothed him with the finest linen, placed a golden necklace on his neck, and made him ascend into his second chariot. Besides all of that, he ordered the people to bow down before Joseph. The wisdom given to Joseph by God was good, not only for preserving the life of the people of Egypt, but especially what would be the life of the people of Israel as well.

One of the classic examples in the Bible of how to obtain wisdom and how wisdom was necessary to help, guide, and judge was that of Solomon. His wisdom attracted people from everywhere: "People from all over came to hear the wisdom of Solomon, from all kings of the earth, who had heard of his wisdom" (1 Kings 4:34). The Bible tells us that after the death of King David, Solomon was confirmed as king, and he summoned the people of Israel to the high place in Gibeon, for there was the Tabernacle of the congregation and the Brazen Altar that Bezalel had made about 620 years before, and how Solomon went before the Lord and offered a thousand burnt offerings (2 Chronicles 1:6). According to Finis Jennings Dake, in his *Dake's Annotated Reference Bible*, the contemporary cost of the offering probably was about $325,000 if the offering were made of bulls at $325 each, or $20,000 if the offering were made of lambs, goats, or rams at $20 each, plus the cost of flour, wine, and oil needed for each sacrifice.[4] Solomon probably selected a thousand bulls because that would have reflected his royal magnificence.

The Bible shows Solomon's love for the Lord God by speaking about his obedience towards God's commandments (1 Kings 3:3). Therefore, it should not be strange to us to see him calling the people of Israel into Gibeon to burn offerings unto God. And it is interesting to notice that it is at the Brazen Altar and the Tabernacle of Congregation built by Bezalel in Gibeon where Solomon offers these sacrifices. Bezalel built these about 680 years[5] after being filled with wisdom to lead the construction of the Tabernacle. I am sure that Solomon was aware of the capabilities given by God to Bezalel and of the kind of work that was done. That same night, God said to Solomon in a dream, "Ask what I might give to you" (2 Chronicles 1:7). And Solomon said unto Him, "Now give wisdom and knowledge to me so that I might know how to go before this people, for who can judge this great people of Yours?" (2 Chronicles 1:10).

We have seen that Solomon loved God and was obedient to His commandments. Being obedient to God's commandments meant to know and to study them, recognizing that it is God who gives wisdom. Therefore, Solomon understood that he needed the wisdom and knowledge to govern and judge the people accordingly. God was so pleased with Solomon's request that He gave him much more than what he asked for (Ephesians 3:20):

> Then God responded to Solomon, "Because this was in your heart and you did not ask for possessions, wealth, and honor, or even the life of those who hate you, nor have you asked for many days of life, but you have asked Me for wisdom and knowledge that you might govern My people over whom I have made you king, wisdom and knowledge are now given to you. Possessions, wealth, and honor I will also give to you; such has not been given to kings before you nor those who will follow after you." (2 Chronicles 1:11–12)

In 1 King 3:14, God grants Solomon longevity if he remains obedient to His commandments. In summary, God gives Solomon wisdom, knowledge, riches, properties, glory, honor, and long life.

It was not a long time before he faced an opportunity to confirm the wisdom given by God before others. The first challenge listed by the Word of God for King Solomon was the one of the two prostitutes who came before him, one accusing the other of exchanging her live child for the other's dead child while she was asleep. Not knowing who was telling the truth, the king asked for a sword, and he ordered the living child be cut in two, with one half given to one woman and the other half to the other. At once, the real mother of the child asked for clemency from the king: "Give her the living child, and do not slay it. She is its mother" (1 Kings 3:27). The Scriptures say, "All Israel heard of the king's judgment, and they feared the king, for they saw that the wisdom of God was in him, to execute sound judgment" (1 Kings 3:28).

Solomon's wisdom expanded throughout the whole earth, and when the Queen of Sheba heard about his fame, she came to see him and test him with difficult questions, of which the Word says were all answered, "When the queen of Sheba observed Solomon's wisdom and the house he had built and the meat of his table and the sitting of his servants and the attendance of his ministers and their clothing and his cupbearers and his entryway by which he went up to the house of the Lord, it took her breath away" (1 Kings 10:4–5).

If we analyze these verses, we can see that Queen of Sheba, besides being impressed with the spiritual details, as it was the Holocaust, was amazed not only by the construction, but by the artistic elements found within the house, the different rooms, and even with the garments of those who served. She recognized that whatever she had heard was not even half of she had been told. However, her astonishment was not just centered on Solomon's wisdom, riches, and beautiful possessions. The Bible tells us that the queen called blessed all of the servants who were continuously before Solomon, listening to his wisdom (1 Kings 10:8). But even more, she praised and glorified in the name of the Lord: "Blessed be the Lord your God, who delighted in you and set you on the throne of Israel, because the Lord loved Israel forever; therefore He made you king in order to execute judgment and justice" (1 Kings 10:9).

Daniel is another example of an individual in whom God poured His Spirit of wisdom. Daniel recognized that wisdom comes from God, and he thanked Him for it:

Daniel answered and said:

"Blessed be the name of God forever and ever,
   for wisdom and might are His. It is He who changes the
times and the seasons;
   He removes kings and sets up kings;
He gives wisdom to the wise
   and knowledge to those who know understanding.
He reveals the deep and secret things;
   He knows what is in the darkness,
   and the light dwells with Him.
I thank and praise You, O God of my fathers;
   for You have given me wisdom and might,
and have made known to me now what we asked of You,
   for You have made known to us the king's matter."
(Daniel 2:20–23)

Incidentally, those who witnessed how the spirit of wisdom moved in Daniel would also refer to it as the spirit of excellence, or an excellent spirit. In Chapter 5 of the book of Daniel, we see that

King Belshazzar prepared a banquet in which he used the silver and gold glasses that King Nebuchadnezzar brought from the temple in Jerusalem, and with them, "They drank wine and praised the gods of gold and of silver, of bronze, of iron, of wood, and of stone" (Daniel 5:4). In the same hour, the hand of a man came forth, writing on the wall, which troubled the king, for he did not understand what it said. The king cried aloud to bring in the astrologers, the Chaldeans, and the soothsayers. And the king said to the wise men of Babylon, "Whoever shall read this writing and show me its interpretation shall be clothed with scarlet and have a chain of gold about his neck and shall be the third ruler in the kingdom" (Daniel 5:7). Despite the promises offered, no one was able to interpret the writing. But the queen had heard about Daniel:

> There is a man in your kingdom in whom is the Spirit of the Holy God. And, in the days of your father, light and understanding and wisdom (*chokmah*), like the wisdom of the gods, were found in him. And King Nebuchadnezzar, your father, your father the king, made him master of the magicians, astrologers, Chaldeans, and soothsayers. Inasmuch as an excellent spirit and knowledge and understanding, interpreting dreams and explanation of enigmas and solving of problems, were found in the same Daniel, whom the king named Belteshazzar, now let Daniel be called, and he will give the interpretation. Then Daniel was brought in before the king. And the king spoke and said to Daniel, "Are you that Daniel who is one of the sons of the captivity of Judah, whom the king my father brought out of Judah? Now I have heard of you, that the Spirit of God is in you; and that light, and understanding, and excellent (*yattiyr*) wisdom have been found in you. (Daniel 5:11–14, emphasis added)

The original word for "greater" and "abundance" comes from the Aramaic *yattiyr*[6] and means "extraordinary," or "excellent"; in other words, they knew that there was an excellent spirit in Daniel, a spirit much more excellent or a spirit of excellence, a spirit of a superior quality compared to everything they had seen before. Thus, we can see how the spirit of excellence is attached to the spirit of wisdom, which comes from the Spirit of God.

Daniel was able to interpret the writing on the wall, and on that same night, King Belshazzar was slain, and Darius of Median took the kingdom, which brought confirmation to Daniel's interpretation. Darius started to reorganize the kingdom, and he set 120 princes over his whole kingdom and established three presidents, of whom Daniel was one. And the Bible continues to say, "Then this Daniel was preferred above the presidents and officials because an excellent spirit was in him, and the king thought to set him over the whole realm" (Daniel 6:3).

We can see how wisdom enlightened Joseph for the preservation of life and to rule over a kingdom. It led Solomon to judge and to govern, and it allowed Daniel to interpret the message of God and to instruct governors. And to Bezalel, wisdom led him while constructing the Tabernacle. All of this makes me understand that regardless of the calling, wisdom (*chokmah*) is one of the essential fundaments, and God will be recognized in you by those who surround you.

SEEK WISDOM

God admonishes us through His word to seek and obtain wisdom. Hence, it must be important or essential for us. It is really something that God wants us to "get wisdom!" He says in Proverbs 4:5, "Wisdom is principal; therefore get wisdom" (Proverbs 4:7). The word "obtain" comes from the Hebrew *qanah*,[7] which means to have, to acquire, to purchase, or to possess. Henceforth, obtain wisdom, possess wisdom, and, if necessary, buy wisdom. This brings to memory Proverbs 23:23: "Buy the truth (*qanah*), and do not sell it." Moreover, wisdom seeks us, calls us, and claims us, especially if you are among the ones who lack wisdom, meaning, wisdom is looking for the sensible or those who lack it:

Wisdom cries out in the street;
 she utters her voice in the markets.
She cries at the corner of the streets, in the openings of the

gates;
    she speaks her words in the city, saying:
  "How long, you simple ones, will you love simplicity?
  For the scorners delight in their scorning,
  and fools hate knowledge." (Proverbs 1:20–22)

The search for and claim of wisdom by us, Solomon tells the author of the book of Proverbs, is through different places. You have to be vigilant in the seeking. Search in different places (mentors, books, the Bible). Therefore, we have no excuse for not finding wisdom, because wisdom itself becomes accessible to us:

  Does not wisdom cry out,
    and understanding lift up her voice?
  She stands on the top of high places,
    by the way in the places of the paths.
  She cries out at the gates,
    at the entry of the city, at the entrance of the doors:
  "To you, O men, I call,
    and my voice is to the sons of men.
  O you simple, understand wisdom,
    and you fools, be of an understanding heart. (Proverbs 8:1–5)

Solomon continues, saying that wisdom not only seeks us with a claim, but it has also sent its servants:

  Wisdom has built her house,
  she has hewn out her seven pillars;

  She has sent out her maidens,
  she cries out from the highest places of the city,
  "Whoever is simple, let him turn in here."
  As for him who wants understanding, she says to him. (Proverbs 9:1, 3–4)

I understand, then, that not only God gives the spirit of wisdom, but that wisdom itself seeks us. Maybe this is just poetic imagery used by Solomon, but the passages emphasize God's desire for us to obtain wisdom. It looks to me like a beautiful image that is letting us know that wisdom is really at our reach. It is not for any particular group; neither is it for a person full of academic awards. On the contrary, these passages emphasize and call on the simple: "How long, you simple ones, will you love simplicity?" (Proverbs 1:22a). And the Scripture repeats, "Whoever is simple, let him turn in here" (Proverbs 9:4a). For that reason, there are no excuses. Wisdom becomes accessible to all who love her and really desire to obtain her: "I love those who love me, and those who seek me early will find me" (Proverbs 8:17).

WHO GIVES WISDOM

Everything that the Bible says about wisdom seems very desirable. I long for wisdom, the one that God gives: "He lays up sound wisdom for the righteous; He is a shield to those who walk uprightly" (Proverbs 2:7). I put emphasis on the wisdom that God gives because, while I read the book of James, I found out that there are two different types of wisdom: spiritual wisdom and demonic wisdom. Concerning demonic wisdom, the book says, "But if you have bitter envying and strife in your hearts, do not boast and do not lie against the truth. This wisdom descends not from above, but is earthly, unspiritual, and devilish" (James 3:14–15). But concerning spiritual wisdom, it says that he who is wise and with understanding will demonstrate his wisdom through acceptable conduct and meekness: "But the wisdom that is from above is first pure, then peaceable, gentle, open to reason, full of mercy and good fruits, without partiality, and without hypocrisy. And the fruit of righteousness is sown in peace by those who make peace" (James 3:17–18).

WHERE TO FIND WISDOM

We are searching for spiritual wisdom, which James says comes from above, and this is echoed in chapter 28:12 of the book of Job: "But where will wisdom be found?" I believe that if we really knew the value of wisdom for our personal lives and for our art, we would not rest until we found it, but, "Man does not know its price, nor is it found in the land of the living" (verse 13). Once again, I ask, where is it found? Job continues, saying that, this time, it is not found in the land of the living, and neither can it be bought or interchanged for precious jewels:

> The depth says, 'It is not in me,'
>   and the sea says, 'It is not with me.'
> It cannot be bought for gold,
>   nor can silver be weighed for its price.
> It cannot be valued in the gold of Ophir,
>   with the precious onyx or the sapphire.
> The gold and the crystal cannot equal it,
>   and it cannot be exchanged for jewels of fine gold.
> No mention will be made of coral or of pearls,
>   for the price of wisdom is above rubies.
> The topaz of Ethiopia will not equal it,
>   nor will it be valued with pure gold. (Job 28:14–19)

Job continues his quest to answer the question: "Where does wisdom come from?" He understands that it is hidden for all living beings and that is why it must be obtained, which requires certain effort from our side; only God can guide us to wisdom:

> God understands its way,
>   and He knows its place.
> For He looks to the ends of the earth,
>   and sees under the whole heaven,
> to make the weight of the wind,
>   and He weighs the waters by measure.
> When He made a decree for the rain,
>   and a path for the lightning of the thunder,
> then He saw it and declared it;
>   He prepared it, yes, and searched it out. (Job 28:23–27)

Job ends his narration about the search for wisdom by saying that God Himself told man, "'Look, the fear of the Lord, that is wisdom'" (Job 28:28). The same was repeated by David when he wrote: "The fear of the Lord is the beginning of wisdom; all who live it have insight. His praise endures forever!" (Psalms 111:10). Solomon declared once again, "The fear of the Lord is the beginning of wisdom" (Proverbs 9:10), and he added, "The fear of the Lord is to hate evil; pride and arrogance and the evil way and the perverse mouth I hate" (Proverbs 8:13). It is established, then, by the words of these three witnesses that the fear of God is the beginning of all wisdom. Now we need to discover what the fear of God is. Solomon helps to understand it:

> My son, if you will receive my words,
>   and hide my commandments within you,
> so that you incline your ear to wisdom,
>   and apply your heart to understanding;
> yes, if you cry out for knowledge,
>   and lift up your voice for understanding,
> if you seek her as silver,
>   and search for her as for hidden treasures,
> then you will understand the fear of the Lord,
>   and find the knowledge of God.
> For the Lord gives wisdom;
>   out of His mouth come knowledge and understanding.
> He lays up sound wisdom for the righteous;
>   He is a shield to those who walk uprightly. (Proverbs 2:1–7)

The word "fear" comes from the Hebrew *yir'ah*,[8] which means reverence. It is this reverence, veneration, love, and respect unto God that makes us wise. Loving God is manifested by being attentive to His voice and by keeping His word. When you love, you pay attention to all that your beloved says or does, and it becomes your utmost pleasure to please and demonstrate to that beloved how important he is to you. Solomon himself was a witness to it: "Solomon loved the Lord, walking in the statutes of his father David" (1 Kings 3:3). He experienced the wisdom that can be obtained by diligently studying the Word of God. For that reason, I believe that when the Lord spoke to him in his dreams, telling him to ask for whatever he wanted, Solomon had a foundation. He loved God, was obedient to His Word, and knew that "wisdom is given by God"; he knew that wisdom is part of the Spirit of God. He had to realize that as soon as God agreed to his request in his dream, wisdom would be made manifest in his life. I am sure that Solomon was the first one to amaze himself, saying, "This must have been the Lord because it would have never occurred to me." If we go back to the case of the two prostitutes and the child, we notice that Solomon did not have time to make an investigation or have some DNA taken. God, through the process, brought the thought to his mind, which is the illumination that comes and tells you what to do when you do not know what to do.

The question is: where can this wisdom be found? The Bible tells us, "With Him are wisdom and strength; He has counsel and understanding" (Job 12:13). How can we find it? How can we obtain it? As an answer to these questions, the book of James says, "If any of you lacks wisdom, let him ask of God, who gives to all men liberally and without criticism, and it will be given to him. But let him ask in faith, without wavering. For he who wavers is like a wave of the sea, driven and tossed with the wind" (James 1:5–6). It is interesting to note that fear or reverence unto the Lord and the search for wisdom become an ascendant circular movement where the fear of God is the beginning of wisdom. It is when you obtain wisdom that you really understand the fear of God in a more profound way. The fear of God is the beginning of wisdom, but to be able to understand it, you must seek, desire, and learn wisdom.

Proverbs 3:1 says, "My son, do not forget my teaching, but let your heart keep my commandments," and Proverbs 4:10 says, "Hear, my son, and receive my sayings." Thus, wisdom can be found in knowing and keeping the Word of God, and that knowledge of the Word reveals to us fear and reverence unto God. The greater the fear and reverence unto God, the greater the search and the study of the Word. It is not a passive step, but one that requires effort and study. Therefore, wisdom originates in God and emerges through the study of His word, and His word takes us to Him.

The Word of God is light. Thus, it enlightens me, and it makes me see the things that I cannot see in the darkness: "The giving of Your words gives light; it grants understanding to the simple" (Psalm 119:130). When you do not know what to do since ignorance is like darkness, the answers could be facing you, but if it is dark, you cannot see; you do not know what to do. For that reason, light is like wisdom: "To the upright there arises light in the darkness" (Psalm 112:4a). The Word of God goes before me and enlightens my path: "Your word is a lamp to my feet and a light to my path" (Psalm 119:105). Wisdom makes you shine like light is coming from you: "Who is like a wise man? And who knows the interpretation of a matter? A man's wisdom makes his face shine, and the harshness of his face is softened" (Ecclesiastes 8:1).

BENEFITS OF WISDOM

Wisdom promises, among other things, to keep us, protect us, promote us, give us honor, give us grace before others, and give us many years of life:

> Wisdom is principal; therefore get wisdom.
>   And with all your getting, get understanding.
> Exalt her, and she will promote you;
>   she will bring you honor, when you embrace her.
> She will place on your head an ornament of grace;
>   a crown of glory she will deliver to you."
>
> Hear, my son, and receive my sayings,
>   and the years of your life will be many. (Proverbs 4:7–10)

If we exalt and honor wisdom, if we give her a place of prominence and respect in our lives, she will, in turn, promote us, keep us, and give us honor.

Besides all that has been mentioned before, the Bible says that happy is the man who finds wisdom (Proverbs 3:13). Obtaining wisdom is better than riches, for it gives much more than riches. Wisdom continuously emphasizes that it gives honor and a long life with comfort and peace, and one still full of riches:

> For her benefit is more profitable than silver,
>   and her gain than *fine* gold.
> She is more precious than rubies,

and all the things you may desire are not to be compared
with her.
Length of days is in her right hand,
  and in her left hand riches and honor.
Her ways are ways of pleasantness,
  and all her paths are peace.
She is a tree of life to those who take hold of her,
  and happy is everyone who retains her. (Proverbs 3:14–
18)

It is ironic to find some who will discard wisdom from their
lives to search for riches, but the Bible tells us that he who searches
for wisdom will also find riches with it. Wisdom is delicious,
pleasant, and enjoyable; it is good, and it produces trust:

Incline your ear and hear the words of the wise,
  and apply your heart to my knowledge;
for it is a pleasant thing if you keep them within you;
  they will readily be fitted in your lips.
That your trust may be in the Lord,
  I have made known to you this day, even to you.
(Proverbs 22:17–19)

Wisdom helps me to obtain success. It will be my reward,
and it will do me good; my hope will have a future, for it will not
be spoiled, and it is emphasized once again that wisdom is as good
and sweet as honey:

if you say, "Surely we did not know this,"
  does not He who ponders the heart consider it?
And He who keeps your soul, does He not know it?
  And will He not render to every man according to his
works?

My son, eat honey because it is good,
  and the honeycomb that is sweet to your taste;
so shall the knowledge of wisdom be to your soul;
  when you have found it, then there will be a reward,
  and your expectation will not be cut off. (Proverbs 24:12–

14)

The book of Proverbs continuously reminds us about the benefits of wisdom, as we saw before with Joseph, Solomon, and Daniel; wisdom allows us to govern, to judge, and to do it boldly and consistently:

> By me kings reign,
>   and princes decree justice.
> By me princes rule,
>   and nobles, even all the judges of the earth.
>
> ………
> Riches and honor are with me,
>   yes, enduring riches and righteousness.
> My fruit is better than gold,
>   yes, than fine gold, and my revenue than choice silver.
> I lead in the way of righteousness,
>   in the midst of the paths of justice, (Proverbs 8:15–16, 18–20)

Moreover, wisdom promises us that whoever keeps it, treasures it, loves it, and protects it – which implies holding wisdom in high esteem, searching for it, yearning for it – she will reward him by giving life and the Lord 's favor. Nevertheless, for those who do not love and appreciate wisdom, not to love wisdom is like loving death:

> "Now therefore listen to me, O you children,
>   for blessed are those who keep my ways…
>
> Blessed is the man who hears me,
>   watching daily at my gates,
>   waiting at the posts of my doors.
> For whoever finds me finds life,
>   and will obtain favor of the Lord;
> but he who sins against me wrongs his own soul;
>   all those who hate me love death." (Proverbs 8:32, 34–36)

And, Solomon continues, saying of the man who goes astray or who departs from the path of wisdom, "The man who wanders out of the way of understanding will remain in the congregation of the dead" (Proverbs 21:16). On the other hand, to have wisdom is to have many years of life: "For by me your days will be multiplied, and the years of your life will be increased" (Proverbs 9:11).

Furthermore, Scripture tells us that, "Wisdom is better than strength" (Ecclesiastes 9:16). If we know what we have to do, not only will we avoid adding physical strength to the work or project that we are working on, but psychological, emotional, and mental strength as well. Wisdom allows us to build our house, and here the concept of a house is symbolic. The house could be our job, our career, our vocation, or just a mere project. "Through wisdom is a house built, and by understanding it is established" (Proverbs 24:3). Ecclesiastes 10:10 tells us, "If an iron piece is blunt and there is no one to sharpen it, then he must prevail with more strength; but wisdom is a benefit to succeed." If we concentrate during the first phase of a project, when all the plans are being set, and we ask for wisdom at the time of getting to work on the project, everything will move smoothly and with promptness, all because, during that first phase, we considered all aspects of the project and we will have the wisdom to catch possible mistakes, errors, and challenges, bringing them to correction in time. It is very important not to accelerate the planning period of a project, but, above all, to seek wisdom, to dedicate some time to praying, thinking, and meditating on it. It is the only way to make the necessary adjustments: "The wisdom of the prudent is to understand his way, but the folly of fools is deceit" (Proverbs 14:8). Wisdom is to know what you have to do and when to do it. Wisdom will help you to accomplish more in less time. Wisdom helps you to be successful in all your endeavors, in all your art projects.

Wisdom is knowing what to do when you do not know what to do. When you face a group of actors and all of a sudden you do not know how to solve the scenery movement because the stage is bigger or smaller than stipulated, or how to find out what is not properly functioning within the set or scene, it is then when wisdom, which is not knowledge but the ability to use knowledge, tells you what you have to do.

Obtaining wisdom through the Word of God makes our jobs easier. When man sinned and fell from the grace of God, everything got complicated, even the way of doing our jobs: "In the sweat of your face you shall eat bread, till you return unto the ground" (Genesis 3:19). However, in Luke 5, Jesus tells Peter to cast the nets into the sea, and Peter answers that they were fishing all night and caught nothing. But then he says, "Master we have worked all night and have caught nothing, but in your name, I will cast out the nets." Having said that, they caught a multitude of fishes, so many that the nets were breaking; the words of wisdom given by Jesus made the job easier.

FOR WHOM IS THE WISDOM?

If wisdom is obtained by the fear of God and by the study of His word, it means that it is reserved for those who love God; it is reserved for us:

He lays up sound wisdom for the righteous;
  He is a shield to those who walk uprightly.
He keeps the paths of justice,
  and preserves the way of His saints.

Then you will understand righteousness and judgment
  and equity, and every good path.
When wisdom enters your heart,
  and knowledge is pleasant to your soul,
discretion will preserve you;
  understanding will keep you,
to deliver you from the way of the evil man,
  from the man who speaks perverse things, (Proverbs 2:7–12)

It is interesting to note how wisdom is always accompanied by justice. If we take a quick look at the book of Isaiah 11, where it speaks about the spirit of wisdom, in verses 3–4, it says "and he shall not judge after the sight of his eyes, neither reprove after the hearing of his ears; but with righteousness shall he judge the poor."

As born-again children of God, wisdom is already ours since, in Christ Jesus, we are justified, but the Bible also says that Jesus became wisdom for us, and if we are in Christ, then we have all of its attributes. That means that I am wise because God, through Jesus, made me wise. "But because of Him you are in Christ Jesus, whom God made unto us wisdom, righteousness, sanctification, and redemption" (1 Corinthians 1:30). Therefore, wisdom is at my disposal, it is stored for me, and I am wise in Christ Jesus. But even though the Bible says that I am wise in Christ Jesus, this does not exonerate me from studying and seeking wisdom, but I understand that I must study and seek wisdom in a positive way. I must study and seek the wisdom that was given to me and activate that which is already mine. This is the opposite of studying from a negative perspective, without any hope, or thinking that we cannot reach wisdom because we lack advance studies or because we do not have what it takes.

God wants to give us wisdom, and through His Word, He teaches us how to obtain it. Bezalel obtained it when he was called and filled with the Spirit of God and wisdom. Job, David, and Solomon tell us that the beginning of all wisdom is the fear of God, and Proverbs shows the Word of God as the way to obtain wisdom. Solomon asked God for wisdom, Joshua the son of Nun, was filled with wisdom because Moses placed his hands upon him (Deuteronomy 34:9), and the apostle Paul says that, by God, we are made wise in Christ Jesus (1 Corinthians 1:30).

Notes:

[1]James Strong, LL.D., S.T.D., *The New Strong's Expanded Exhaustive Concordance of the Bible,* (Nashville: Thomas Nelson, 2010), 87.

[2]_____, *The New Strong's Expanded Exhaustive Concordance of the Bible,* (Nashville: Thomas Nelson, 2010), 87.

[3](https://www.psychologytoday.com/us/blog/hide-and-seek/201811/what-is-wisdom)

[4]Finis Jennings Dake, *Dake's Annotated Reference Bible,* (Georgia, Dake Publishing, Inc., 2014), 621.

[5] _____, *Dake's Annotated Reference Bible*, (Georgia, Dake Publishing, Inc., 2014), 750.

[6] James Strong, LL.D., S.T.D., *The New Strong's Expanded Exhaustive Concordance of the Bible*, (Nashville: Thomas Nelson, 2010), 124.

[7] _____, *The New Strong's Expanded Exhaustive Concordance of the Bible*, (Nashville: Thomas Nelson, 2010), 248.

[8] _____, *The New Strong's Expanded Exhaustive Concordance of the Bible*, (Nashville: Thomas Nelson, 2010), 120.

CHAPTER 3

UNDERSTANDING
Creative Discernment

> I have filled him with the Spirit of
> God in wisdom, in understanding.
> (Exodus 31:3)

DISTINGUISHING THE TRUE FROM THE FALSE

This is one of my favorite words; with wisdom and understanding, you become unstoppable. And the Lord knows it, so He included it in the powerful gifts package He gave to Bezalel: "I have filled him with the Spirit of God in wisdom, in understanding," (Exodus 31:3c). We have already seen two of the gifts bestowed to Bezalel: the Spirit of God and wisdom; now He's added understanding. So, let's explore the meaning and benefits of understanding and how to make it our own.

"Understanding" is a word that comes from the Hebrew *tabuwn*.[1] Usually, it is translated into "intelligence" or "comprehension." To those who like to explore the meaning of specific keywords in the Hebrew because it enhances the interpretation of the verse, I want to make you aware that there is another Hebrew word for understanding: *biynah*.[2] The word *tabuwn*, as well as the word *biynah*, come from the Hebrew root *biyn*,[3] which means "intelligence, to mentally separate, distinguish, comprehend, consider, discern, inform, instruct, understand, know, perceive, teach, think, and/or to be of prudence."

According to Webster's Dictionary, understanding is comprehension, or in other words, the act or action of grasping with the intellect. Other biblical translations interpret the word *tabuwn* as "intelligence." And according to Webster's Dictionary, intelligence is the act of knowing or comprehending, being able to know the information; even the dictionary sees intelligence as a gift or donation. An intelligent person is a fitted person, a person skilled to know or discern the difference between truth or deception. It is a person able to interpret or explain knowledge about art or any other subject. The Encyclopedia Britannica defines intelligence as "mental quality," which consists of the capacity to learn from the experience, to adapt to new situations, to comprehend and deal with abstract concepts, and to utilize knowledge to manipulate surroundings. God gave Bezalel the gift of understanding /intelligence to solve the problems that he would face during the construction of the Tabernacle.

The artist needs to have the capacity to solve complex issues. For example, when I direct a play, I have the responsibility to read the script and interpret it artistically. For this, I need to do a play analysis. I need to know about the given circumstances, dialogue, dramatic action, meaning of the title, and what the play is all about, among other things, to discover the intention of the writer and to know how to transmit it to the public. I am sure that although God had given the blueprint or design of the Tabernacle to Moses, Bezalel confronted situations where he had to apply his knowledge about metals, wood, and design interpretation and discern if he had any artistic freedom and what his limits were.

The fact that God spoke to Moses concerning the capabilities that He had bestowed upon Bezalel is, to me, motivation to keep researching. What do words such as "wisdom" and "understanding" contain that God specifically mentioned them concerning Bezalel? When God told Moses, "And I have filled him...in understanding (*tabuwn*)," I recognize that understanding, like wisdom, is also a gift from God but that it requires, like wisdom, a serious search. In addition to the desire to obtain understanding, it requires effort and dedication. Such a search will take us to God because, in Him, is the understanding:

> Yes, if you cry out for knowledge,
>   and lift up your voice for understanding,
> if you seek her as silver,
>   and search for her as for hidden treasures,
> then you will understand the fear of the Lord,
>   and find the knowledge of God.
> For the Lord gives wisdom;
>   out of His mouth come knowledge and understanding.
> (Proverbs 2:3–6).

Continuing our study, we find in the Holy Scriptures that understanding can be achieved through the study of the Word of God: "Through Your precepts I receive understanding; therefore I hate every false way" (Psalm 119:104). We gain understanding through the Word of God. Solomon exhorts us to reach out for wisdom. However, he emphasizes that, with it, we must obtain understanding: "Get wisdom! Get understanding! ... Wisdom is principal; therefore get wisdom. And with all your getting, get understanding" (Proverbs 4:5, 7). Remember that obtaining understanding is more precious than silver (Proverbs 16:16) and that not only is there an intellectual benefit, but "He who gets wisdom loves his own soul; he who keeps understanding, find good" (Proverbs 19:8). Once you have obtained wisdom, do not sell it: "Buy the truth, and do not sell it, also wisdom and instruction and understanding" (Proverbs 23:23).

WHERE TO FIND UNDERSTANDING

It is interesting to note that through his declaration, Job, when he speaks about understanding, not only asks himself where could it be found, but he also inquiries about prudence, which is another aspect of understanding in some translations: "But where shall wisdom be found? And where is the place of understanding [*biynah*]?" (Job 28:12). It is as if they would be hidden and we would have to know who has them and where we could go find them. Almost towards the end of his speech on wisdom, Job says, "God understands its way, and He knows its place" (Job 28:23). Then the solution is in God, and it is then that Job reveals what God has said: "To man He said: 'Look, the fear of the Lord, that is wisdom; And to depart from evil is understanding'" (Job 28:28). Moses tells the people of Israel, speaking about the laws and decrees which he had taught them about, "Therefore, keep and do *them*, for this is your wisdom and your understanding in the sight of the nations which shall hear all these statutes, and say, 'Surely this great nation is a wise and understanding people'" (Deuteronomy 4:6). To keep the Word of God makes me a wise and understanding person, and it makes me intelligent. We acquire understanding from the commandments of God, and everything against them is called deceit by the Psalmist when he says, "Through Your precepts I receive understanding; therefore I hate every false way" (Psalms 119:104).

When we meditate on the Word of God, it produces understanding about all hidden things:

> My mouth will speak wisdom,
>   and the meditation of my heart will be understanding.
> I will incline my ear to a parable;
>   I will expound my riddle with a harp.
> (Psalms 49:3–4)

The Hebrew word for "thought" is *haguwth*,[4] which also means meditation. But what is meditation? It seems to be key in the process of obtaining understanding. When one investigates, one finds that the Hebrew word for meditation is *hagah*,[5] which means to murmur, to reflect about, imagine, to sob, to quarrel, to speak of. When one meditates on the Word, one speaks it and repeats it over and over until one gets understanding. This will help us to understand and solve the secrecy, or the mystery, of that which I do not know.

BENEFITS OF UNDERSTANDING

As a consequence of asking for understanding, God tells Solomon:

> Then God said to him: "Because you have asked this thing, and have not asked long life for yourself, nor have asked riches for yourself, nor have asked the life of your enemies, **but have asked for yourself understanding [*biyn*] to discern justice**, behold, I have done according to your words; see, I have given you a wise and **understanding [biyn] heart**, so that there has not been anyone like you before you, nor shall any like you arise after you. And I have also given you what you have not asked: both riches and honor, so that there shall not be anyone like you among the kings all your days. So if you walk in My ways, to keep My statutes and My commandments, as your father David walked, then I will lengthen your days" (1 Kings 3:11–14, NKJV, emphasis added)

And the MEV translates this as "but have asked for yourself **wisdom [biyn]** so that you may have **discernment in judging**." It seems that this specific wisdom or understanding that comes from the root word (biyn) is closely linked with the word "justice," or "judgment." It is not the wisdom that comes from ability; it's the wisdom that comes from **biyn**, from the ability to discern between good and evil; in other words, Solomon was going to have discernment.

This calls my attention to what God tells him: "**But have asked for yourself understanding to discern justice.**" The word "asked" is the Hebrew word *sha'al*,[6] which means "to request, to demand." Solomon's asking went beyond a simple prayer or desire. To request speaks about supplication, about pleading, and this is a petition that reached the Lord with a strong emotional burden because he was asking for understanding to judge, to choose between what was just and what was not, and to judge with righteousness is in God's heart.

I am assured that Solomon understood the deep meaning of wisdom and its connection to justice, as we see it in 1King 3:9: "Give Your servant therefore an **understanding heart to judge** Your people, that I may discern between good and bad, for who is able to judge among so great a people?" (emphasis added) Maybe he already confronted some situations where he did not know what to do. Maybe he witnessed moments where King David did not know what to do. I also know that although God visited Solomon in his dreams, the spirit never sleeps, and his spirit was able to answer God's request: "Ask what you want from Me" (1Kings 3:5b). God was able to see Solomon's heart and his request to judge with integrity.

As a side note, I can see the connection between wisdom, understanding, and judgment when the prophet Isaiah prophesied about the seven spirits that would rest upon Jesus:

> The Spirit of the Lord shall rest upon him,
>   the Spirit of wisdom and understanding,
>   the Spirit of counsel and might,
>   the Spirit of knowledge and of the fear of the Lord.
>
> He shall delight in the fear of the Lord. (Isaiah 11:2–3a)

And one of the results of these seven spirits will be righteous judgment:

> And he shall **not judge** by what his eyes see,
>   nor **reprove by what his ears hear**;
> but with **righteousness he shall judge the poor**,
>   and **reprove with fairness** for the meek of the earth.
> He shall strike the earth with the rod of his mouth,
>   and with the breath of his lips he shall slay the wicked.
> **Righteousness** shall be the belt of his loins,
>   and **faithfulness** the belt about his waist.
> (Isaiah 11:3b–5, emphasis added)

Understanding preserves and keeps one from danger and harm: "Discretion will preserve you; understanding [tabuwn] will keep you "(Proverbs 2:11). That is why the author of Proverbs recommends maintaining an intimate relationship with understanding: "Say to wisdom, 'You are my sister,' and call understanding your kinswoman" (Proverbs 7:4b). This relationship will be beneficial: "He who gets wisdom [tabuwn] loves his own soul; he who keeps understanding will find good" (Proverbs 19:8). Everything will be good because all one has to do is make the right decision and the satisfaction of that decision will make you glad: "Happy is the man who finds wisdom, and the man who gets understanding" (Proverbs 3:13).

It caught my attention that the Spanish version (RVR 1960) also translates "understanding" as "prudence": "*Y Dios dio a Salomón sabiduría y prudencia muy grandes, y anchura de corazón como la arena que está a la orilla del mar*" (And God gave Solomon wisdom and great prudence, and width of heart like the sand that is at the seashore). Understanding also produces prudence (carefulness, caution). Prudence is the exercise of good judgment to avoid complications and difficulties. The way I treat artists who work with me prevents a lot of disagreements and prepares the environment for collaboration. Looking at other translations, "God gave Solomon wisdom and great depth of understanding as well as compassion, as vast as the sand on the seashore" (1 Kings 4:29 MEV) and "God gave Solomon unusual wisdom and insight, and knowledge too great to be measured" (GNT). Insight talks about having a clear, deep, and sudden understanding of a complicated problem or situation. I need all of the above.

UNDERSTANDING AND CREATION

I find that understanding, just like wisdom, is present in the process of the creation of the world. "The Lord by wisdom has founded the earth; by understanding He has established the heavens" (Proverbs 3:19). The prophet Jeremiah confirms that God "has made the earth by His power. He has established the world by His wisdom (*chokmah*) and has stretched out the heavens by His discretion (*tabuwn*)" (Jeremiah 10:12) and "He has made the earth by His power; He has established the world by His wisdom (*chokmah*), and has stretched out the heaven by His understanding (*tabuwn*)" (Jeremiah 51:15). This is serious, folks! The Lord, talking through the prophet Jeremiah, explained twice, on different occasions and using the same words, *chokmah* (wisdom) and *tabuwn* (discretion, understanding), how He established the world during the process of creation. Let's pray for wisdom and understanding so our artistic works can be established and stretched. This speaks to me about an artwork that is well-founded, well-known, and spread around the word.

UNDERSTANDING AND THE ARTS

Understanding is also associated with art. However, we see here three different examples in the use of understanding. Hiram, king of Tyre, blessed the Lord God of Israel, recognizing Solomon's wisdom and understanding to build the house of God: "And Hiram said, 'Blessed be the Lord God of Israel who made heaven and earth and has given King David a wise son, having insight and understanding, who is building a temple for the Lord and a royal house for his kingship'" (2 Chronicles 2:12). As a result of such a declaration, he sent an artist by the name of Huram-Abi, who was endued with understanding and skill to work in metals, wood, and fabric; he was also an engraver and a designer:

And now I have sent a skilled man, endowed with understanding, Huram-Abi, the son of a woman from the daughters of Dan and the son of a man of Tyre, who knows gold, silver, bronze, iron, stone, wood, and purple, violet, blue, and crimson threads, and who knows how to make all types of engravings and to devise every type of design that is given to him, with your skilled men and the skilled men of my lord David your father. (2 Chronicles 2:13–14)

As a contrast, we have the testimony of the prophet Hosea:

And now they continue sinning
    and have made a cast image for themselves,
    idols of their silver, according to their understanding;

all of them the work of craftsmen.
They say of them,
  "Those who sacrifice
  are kissing calves!" (Hosea 13:2)

Let's look at other translation of the same verse:

> They still keep on sinning by making metal images to worship—idols of silver, designed by human minds, made by human hands. And then they say, "Offer sacrifices to them!" How can anyone kiss those idols—idols in the shape of bulls! (GNT).

And as a consequence, Hosea tells us:

> And so these people will disappear like morning mist, like the dew that vanishes early in the day. They will be like chaff which the wind blows from the threshing place, like smoke from a chimney" (Hosea 13:3).

They used their creativity and initiative to build idols. As opposed to Bezalel, they built idols "according to their own understanding." The concept of idolatry was in the mind and intellect of the builder. The artist devised what the idol was going to represent. He probably debated within himself, rejecting ideas, making different types of decisions, modifying ideas, all according to "his understanding." His understanding thought about it, and the artist constructed it, which brings to my memory what David says:

> Their idols are silver and gold,
>   the work of men's hands.
> They have mouths, but they cannot speak;
>   eyes, but they cannot see;
> they have ears, but they cannot hear;
>   noses, but they cannot smell;
> they have hands, but they cannot feel;
>   feet, but they cannot walk;
>   neither can they speak with their throat.
> Those who make them are like them;
>   so is everyone who trusts in them. (Psalms 115:4–8)

They abused God's gifts, dedicating to idolatry what the Lord had chosen for His use, such as art and natural resources such as silver.

Contrary to these artists, Bezalel received the gift of understanding. This gift can be identified as one of creative discernment that empowered him to distinguish the true from the false. Bezalel had no problem following God's plan. He knew what to do with God's design, what his interpretation limits were, and to whom he needed to submit, and he also knew how to deal with all the people under his direction. One can comprehend here, when you see the difference between the two groups of artists, that the problem was not the art but the intention of the heart. In one case, Bezalel understood that what he was doing was a sanctuary for the Lord God to dwell in; the last group of artists had built a sanctuary for false gods. This understanding in Bezalel empowered him to distinguish between the true and the false. In conclusion, God used art, artists, gold, silver, and precious stones in the Tabernacle, but it was all separated for His glory and beauty (Exodus 28:40).

NOTES

[1] James Strong, LL.D., S.T.D., *The New Strong's Expanded Exhaustive Concordance of the Bible*, (Nashville: Thomas Nelson, 2010), 294.

[2] _____, *The New Strong's Expanded Exhaustive Concordance of the Bible*, (Nashville: Thomas Nelson, 2010), 37.

[3] _____, *The New Strong's Expanded Exhaustive Concordance of the Bible*, (Nashville: Thomas Nelson, 2010), 36.

[4] _____, *The New Strong's Expanded Exhaustive Concordance of the Bible*, (Nashville: Thomas Nelson, 2010), 66.

[5] _____, *The New Strong's Expanded Exhaustive Concordance of the Bible*, (Nashville: Thomas Nelson, 2010), 66.

[6] _____, *The New Strong's Expanded Exhaustive Concordance of the Bible*, (Nashville: Thomas Nelson, 2010), 269.

CHAPTER 4

KNOWLEDGE
Revelation Knowledge

> I have filled him with the Spirit of God
> in wisdom, in understanding, in knowledge.
> *(Exodus 31:3)*

SUPERNATURAL INFORMATION

How beautiful is our God, who does not stop at the count of one, two, or three. For Him, there are no limits. And the training of Bezalel continues. Let's see. The Lord continues to render specifications to Moses, saying, "I have filled him with the Spirit of God in wisdom, in understanding, in knowledge" (Exodus 31:3d). We have already seen three of the gifts given by God to Bezalel: the Spirit of God, wisdom, and understanding; now He adds knowledge.

In the Bible, the word knowledge comes from the Hebrew da'ath,[1] which means "to perceive, being sensitive in sight, touch, and especially in mind." These definitions caught my attention. For example, we know that man is body, soul, and spirit. The body is this covering that God created from the dust of the earth, and since we look at it every day, we have no problem understanding what it is. But we are more than a body; there are a soul and spirit within the body, which the apostle Paul bears witness to when he speaks about the power of the Word of God: "For the word of God is alive, and active, and sharper than any two-edged sword, piercing even to the division of soul and spirit, of joints and marrow, and able to judge the thoughts and intents of the heart" (Hebrews 4:12). In Isaiah 26:9, we begin to see a clear distinction between the soul and the spirit:

> With my soul I have desired You in the night;
>   my spirit within me seeks You diligently;
> for when Your judgments are in the earth,
>   the inhabitants of the world learn righteousness.

The first part of this verse says, "With my soul, I have desired you in the night." Desire is an emotion, and we see how this emotion is expressed through the soul, which is the base of our emotions. The second part of the verse says, "my spirit within me seeks You diligently." Here we see the spirit of man trying to establish communication with God. But how is the spirit of man going to communicate with God? It is in the brain where we can learn, where we keep knowledge, and it is there where we find the capacity to communicate. John the apostle says, "But when the Spirit of truth comes, He will guide you into all truth. For He will not speak on His own authority. But He will speak whatever He hears, and He will tell you things that are to come" (John 16:13). David speaks about a spirit that wants to seek God, and Jesus speaks about sending us His spirit to communicate with us: "And he shall show you the things to come." He will communicate with us, and he will make us understand, think, perceive, and reason. As we continue our study on knowledge, we shall see how it will go beyond just some accumulation of details or information.

Da'ath is also a word or name that comes from the ancient root of the verb yada.[2] It means to know by observation and reflection (thought), but it is also to know through experiencing things with our senses, through investigation and testing. Knowledge deals with the area of education. It is the combination of details, information, facts, or ideas that a person acquires, and this knowledge could be obtained in different ways. It is knowledge received by way of traditional or formal studies, investigation, or life experienced through the use of our five senses; we receive this knowledge by what we see, what we hear, what we touch, what we smell, and what we taste. It is also defined as what we learn through the ability to think, to reason, or even through the information obtained from a subject or area of life.

Bezalel needed to know how to work the wood, to know about the different metals, the precious stones, and how to deal or manage their treatment to be able to get the best result from each one of them. He probably had to observe, experiment, reason, and make an in-depth study of each one. As an artist, I understand that we should be interested in continuing education and developing our talent through observation and reflection, formal studies, or through the knowledge that we get through life experience. Intelligence is a faculty of the mind, while knowledge has to do with the content of the mind.

WHAT THE BIBLE SAYS ABOUT KNOWLEDGE

First of all, it says, "For the Lord gives wisdom; out of His mouth come knowledge and understanding" (Proverbs 2:6); if words come out of His mouth, then knowledge comes from the words spoken by God, and we find His spoken words in the Holy Scriptures. The apostle Paul says that in God the Father and in Christ "are hidden all the treasures of wisdom and knowledge" (Colossians 2:3). If one reads Genesis 1, during the description of the creating process, one notices the phrase "God said" continuously repeated, and then one sees through the whole chapter that everything the Lord said with His words became a reality. As one explores the Bible, especially in reference to knowledge, one sees that knowledge was present during the creation: "By His knowledge the depths are broken up, and the clouds drop down the dew" (Proverbs 3:20). Knowledge is linked to wisdom, and it is greater than silver or gold:

> Receive my instruction, and not silver,
>   and knowledge rather than choice gold;

"I, wisdom, dwell with prudence,
and find out knowledge and discretion. (Proverbs 8:10,
12)

We must strive to obtain knowledge. Learning is not a passive
action:

Apply your heart to instruction,
and your ears to the words of knowledge. (Proverbs
23:12)

However, it is not that God does not want you to have silver,
gold, riches, or wealth; I think that it is a matter of priorities,
because He says:

and by knowledge the rooms will be filled
with all precious and pleasant riches. (Proverbs 24:4)

Just like wisdom (chokmah), knowledge (da'ath) is linked to the
fear of God. Solomon begins the first chapter of Proverbs by saying:

The fear of the Lord is the beginning of knowledge,
but fools despise wisdom and instruction. (Proverbs 1:7)

Proverbs 9:10 says:

The fear of the Lord is the beginning of wisdom
(chokmah), and the knowledge (da'ath) of the Holy One is
understanding (biynah).

REVELATION KNOWLEDGE

What type of knowledge is this? Can this type of knowledge
be manifested in the life of an artist? Since we are talking not only
about the intellectual aspects of art but about the spiritual aspects
as well, I would like to take the concept of knowledge beyond the
natural.

God gives us revelation so that we can go beyond natural
knowledge, or the knowledge obtained through research or

observation. It is the uncovering of that which is hidden that we want to see. It is discovery; it is supernatural information. We could compare it to light and darkness; that type of knowledge is known as revelation knowledge:

> But God has revealed them to us by His Spirit. For the Spirit searches all things, yes, the deep things of God. For what man knows the things of a man, except the spirit of man which is in him? Likewise, no one knows the things of God, except the Spirit of God. Now we have received not the spirit of the world, but the Spirit which is of God, so that we might know the things that are freely given to us by God. (1 Corinthians 2:10–12)

Knowledge comes directly from the Spirit of God and is placed in our spirit, allowing us to operate independently from the knowledge that comes through our senses:

> But as it is written,
> "Eye has not seen,
>   nor ear heard,
> nor has it entered into the heart of man
>   the things which God has prepared for those who love Him." (1 Corinthians 2:9)

In Mathew 16, we see Jesus asking His disciples, "Who do men say that I, the Son of Man, am?" (v. 13). And the different answers come immediately: "Some say that You are John the Baptist, others say Elijah, and others Jeremiah or one of the prophets" (v. 14). Jesus then asks, "But who do you say that I am?" (v. 15) Of course, Peter immediately produces the answer, one that has impacted us until today: "You are the Christ, the Son of the living God" (v. 16). It is at this moment that we see the manifestation of a knowledge that has not been obtained either through observation, reflection, nor the senses: "Blessed are you, Simon son of Jonah, for flesh and blood has not revealed this to you, but My Father who is in heaven" (v. 17). Peter received this knowledge that Jesus was the Christ, the Son of the living God, directly from the Spirit of God into his own spirit.

This is the knowledge that comes directly from the Spirit of God, which, as an artist, I am looking for. When the people of Israel were captives in Babylon, the king requested:

> [To] Ashpenaz the master of his officials that he should bring some of the sons of Israel and some of the king's descendants and some of the nobles, youths in whom was no blemish, who were handsome and skillful in every branch of wisdom and gifted with understanding and discerning knowledge, and such as had ability in them to serve in the king's palace, and whom they might teach the learning and the language of the Chaldeans. (Daniel 1:3–4)

The Bible tells us that Daniel, Hananiah, Mishael, and Azariah were chosen because they had the requirements established by the king. They were wise in all senses of the word. Nevertheless, the Word says that after Daniel purposed in his heart not to defile himself with the portion of the king's meat and agreed with the prince of the eunuchs that all them would not eat the meat either, "At the end of ten days their countenances appeared fairer and fatter than all the youths who ate the portion of the king's food" (Daniel 1:15). The Bible also says, "As for these four youths, God gave them knowledge and skill in every branch of learning and wisdom. And Daniel had understanding in all kinds of visions and dreams" (Daniel 1:17).

If we conduct an analysis of this verse, we find the following: "As for these four youths, God gave them knowledge (madda) and skill." Madda[3] is a word that, just like da'ath, comes from the Hebrew root yada, which speaks about knowledge, but in this case, it refers to an "inner knowledge." It speaks about the capacity to discern between good and evil and know what to do. The Bible says in 2 Chronicles 1:12a that Solomon prayed and asked for wisdom and knowledge and God granted them to him. God granted him that inner knowledge so needed to distinguish good from evil and to know what to do. It is the highest form of communication, from Spirit to spirit; it is the kind of knowledge that we look for.

Secular knowledge is an intellectual and wonderful activity. I constantly enjoy reading and studying about the history of theater, costumes, and drama, but I want more, and I understand that when God spoke to Moses and told him that he had bestowed wisdom and knowledge upon Bezalel, not only was he speaking about knowledge of materials, but about the supernatural knowledge that goes beyond natural senses. This is the knowledge that is obtained from the Holy Spirit. The Spirit of God, just like in the beginning of Creation, when he moved upon the face of the waters, moves upon our spirit giving us perception and spiritual discernment and preparing us for creative action.

THREE KEY WORDS:
WISDOM, UNDERSTANDING, AND KNOWLEDGE

We find that wisdom, understanding, and knowledge are all part of a trilogy of words that are continuously repeated throughout the book of Proverbs and throughout the whole Bible, including the New Testament. This indicates their importance and how they complement and enhance the meaning of each other. In Isaiah 11:2, we see that these words are part of the seven spirits that came upon the Messiah, and if Jesus needed the spirit of wisdom, understanding, and knowledge, how much more do we need them? We have also noted how these are some of the gifts to Bezalel, Oholiab, and all who would participate in the construction of the Tabernacle.

However, it is important to mention that the gifting to Bezalel, Oholiab, and the wise at heart who built the Tabernacle was not exclusively for that historic moment. When King Solomon was ready to build the temple and needed an artist to work at it, the Bible tells us that he called Hiram, the king of Tyre, saying:

> "I am going to build a temple for the name of the Lord my God, sanctified for Him, for making sacrifices before Him, and for incense of fragrant spices, and for the continual

showbread, for burnt offerings on both morning and evening, and for Sabbaths, New Moons, and appointed feasts of the Lord our God, as an ordinance forever for Israel.

"And the house that I am building will be great because our God is greater than all other gods....

"Now may you send to me a wise man who works with gold, silver, bronze, iron, and in purple, crimson, and violet threads and knows how to engrave, who will be with the skilled workers and me in Judah and Jerusalem, which David my father established." (2 Chronicles 2:4–5, 7)

Hiram, the King of Tyre, answered:

"And now I have sent a skilled man, endowed with understanding, Huram-Abi, the son of a woman from the daughters of Dan and the son of a man of Tyre, who knows gold, silver, bronze, iron, stone, wood, and purple, violet, blue, and crimson threads, and who knows how to make all types of engravings and to devise every type of design that is given to him, with your skilled men and the skilled men of my lord David your father." (2 Chronicles 2:13–14)

And we are told:

Now King Solomon sent and called Huram out of Tyre. He was the son of a widow from the tribe of Naphtali, and his father was a man of Tyre who worked in bronze, and he was filled with wisdom and understanding and skill to make all sorts of items in bronze. So he came to King Solomon and performed all his work. (1 Kings 7:13–14)

These three words are continuously seen together, and they often interlace with one another. They are intimately involved with the creative process, whether it is at the moment of Creation, the construction of the Tabernacle, or the building of the Temple of Solomon. In Proverbs 24:3–4, the Word tells us that:

Through wisdom is a house built,
 and by understanding it is established;
and by knowledge the rooms will be filled
 with all precious and pleasant riches.

I do not think that this is referring just to a building, but also to your artistic project. Even more about our artistic project: "Except the Lord build the house, those who build labor in vain" (Psalms 127:1). If the Lord is not the one who edifies, inspires, and builds, my work will be in vain and will not have a solid and transcendental foundation. We want to develop art with significance, value, and impact.

Before moving onto other God-given qualifications to Bezalel, we could say as a way of summarizing things that wisdom is the act of receiving the complete vision of the project, understanding is the act of comprehending the information, distinguishing or discerning between what is true or false, and knowledge is the acquired information. Understanding is a mental faculty we are born with, as opposed to knowledge, which is the content of the mind. Revelation knowledge is knowledge given by the Holy Spirit.

The Holy Spirit is the one who establishes the difference between the natural and the supernatural. It is the Holy Spirit who speaks to your spirit and reveals what you do not know; He gives you the information that is not available to your intellect. He capacitates you supernaturally so that you can use that information to the benefit of the project that you are developing or for the problem that you have to solve.

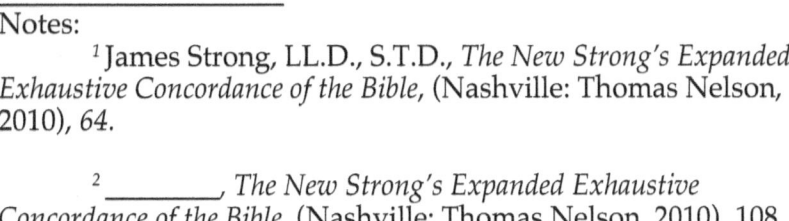

Notes:
 [1] James Strong, LL.D., S.T.D., *The New Strong's Expanded Exhaustive Concordance of the Bible*, (Nashville: Thomas Nelson, 2010), 64.

 [2] _____, *The New Strong's Expanded Exhaustive Concordance of the Bible*, (Nashville: Thomas Nelson, 2010), 108.

 [3] _____, *The New Strong's Expanded Exhaustive Concordance of the Bible*, (Nashville: Thomas Nelson, 2010), 148.

CHAPTER 5

ART
Artistic Creation

> I have filled him with the Spirit of God
> in wisdom, in understanding, in knowledge,
> and in all manner of craftsmanship.
> (Exodus 31:3)

CREATIVITY AND ARTISTIC ABILITY AND TECHNIQUE

WOW! I finally got to the arts! If I had in my hands the decision of how to distribute the gifts, I would have begun with art. But God knows us better, and contrary to what I thought, art is not the first gift He gives to the artist, but the fifth: "I have filled him with the Spirit of God in wisdom, in understanding, in knowledge, and in all manner of craftsmanship" (Exodus 31:3). In other words, the fifth gift is artistic creation. God gave us the gift of his Spirit first; that is, He established Spirit-to-spirit communication first, and then He gave us three other spiritual gifts: wisdom, understanding, and knowledge. In this way, when He finally reveals to us an artistic concept, one is ready to know what to do with what He put in our hands and to be successful.

The word "craftsmanship" comes from the Hebrew *melakah*.[1] I found a variety of translations for this word. And I can imagine that the meaning or interpretation of the word changes depending on how it is used in the sentence. *Melakah* means, among other things, "work (something done or made), hand work, workmanship, occupation, business."[2, 3] It's also translated as "skillful, architect, artist, artisan, artificer, work of art, art."[4] The first time it was used was in Genesis 2:2: "On the seventh day God completed His work (*melakah*) which He had done, and He rested on the seventh day from all His work (*melakah*) which He had done." What work had God completed? The creation of the world. So, the first time *melakah* was used was in the creative process. God's first work was a creative one, an artistic one, that is, a work of art, a masterpiece.

Therefore, if we analyze this word based on the law of first mention, in the context of the kind of "work" that was to be made or the type of "handwork" that was needed, we understand that Exodus 31:3 is talking about creativity, artistic ability, and artistic technique. The Lord told Moses that one of the purposes of the calling and spiritual capability was to "devise [*chashab*, a Hebrew word that I will examine later because it's important to us] artistic works for work with gold, with silver, and with bronze, and in the cutting of stones for settings, and in carving of wood, to work in all manner of craftsmanship" (Exodus 31:4–5). Or, as the Good News Translation (GNT) says, "For planning skillful designs and working them in gold, silver, and bronze; for cutting jewels to be set; for carving wood; and for every other kind of artistic work." According to the job description that appears in Exodus 25 and 28, Moses needed:

- Carpenters
- Designers
- Embroiderers
- Engravers
- Jewelers
- Metalsmiths
- Molders

- Seamstresses
- Weavers
- Woodsmen[5]
- God's team for the construction of the tabernacle consisted of the following people:

1. BEZALEL, an artist, was the chief overseer of the Tabernacle work. He specialized in metal, stone, wood, and apothecary work (Exodus 31:1–5; 37:1, 29)
2. OHOLIAB was Bezalel's assistant and also an artist: "With him was Aholiab...an engraver and designer, an embroiderer in blue and purple and scarlet yarns, and fine linen" (Exodus 38:23).
3. MEN and WOMEN with special abilities to do all manner of work (Exodus 36:1). They crafted parts of the Tabernacle and the garments, among other things. For example:
   a. WOMEN "that were skilled spun with their hands and brought what they had spun, both of blue, purple, and scarlet, and of fine linen. All the women whose hearts stirred them to action and were skilled spun goats' hair" (Exodus 35:25–26).
   b. MEN of skill worked in the sanctuary (Exodus 36:4).
   c. IN GENERAL, "Every skilled craftsman [men & women] among you shall come and make all that the Lord has commanded" (Exodus 35:10, emphasis added).
4. The Lord prepared the team: "He has given them skill in all kinds of work done by engravers [charash], designers [chashab], and weavers [raqam], an embroiderer; a person that mixed colors, a colorist] of fine linen; blue, purple, and red wool; and other cloth. They are able to do all kinds of work and are skillful designers" (Exodus 35:35, GNT). Or as stated in the MEV: "He has filled them with skill to do all manner of work as craftsmen; as designers; as embroiderers in

blue, in purple, in scarlet, and in fine linen; and as weavers: as craftsmen of every work and artistic designers."

There are interesting words here: *charash, chashab*, and *raqam*. It is the first time that the Hebrew word *charash*[6] appears. It means, among other things, "artificer, craftsman, skillful, maker." The word *raqam*[7] means "an embroiderer; a person that mixed colors, a colorist of fine linen; blue, purple, and red wool; and other cloth." All words related in one way or another to the arts. The word *chashab*[8] is even more interesting and important for artists. It means, among other things, "To weave, to fabricate, to imagine, to invent." God called them to weave, to fabricate, to invent, and even to imagine:

- Skillful designs
- Designs in gold, silver, and bronze
- To cut the stones for settings
- To carve wood
- To do all manner of craftsmanship or artistic work

This concept of imagination has been seen as negative in some Christian circles because it's associated with "wicked imaginations" (Proverbs 6:18). Second Corinthians 10:5 says, "Casting down imaginations and every high thing that exalts itself against the knowledge of God, bringing every thought into captivity to the obedience of Christ." There are two different imaginations, one that is creative (*chashab*) and one that is wicked. One can recognize those with wicked imagination by their behavior and fruits:

> This evil people, who refuse to hear My words, who walk in the imagination of their hearts, and walk after other gods, to serve them, and to worship them, shall be even as this waistband which is good for nothing. (Jeremiah 13:10)

> And you have done worse than your fathers, for here you are, each one walking after the imaginations of his evil heart so that they do not listen to Me. (Jeremiah 16:13)

Because, although they knew God, they did not glorify Him or give thanks to Him as God, but became futile in their imaginations, and their foolish hearts were darkened. (Romans 1:21)

But the *chashab* imagination belongs to the wise-hearted men and women, the artists who love the Lord. The dictionary defines imagination as "the ability to come up with mental images of something that is not real or to come up with new and creative ideas."[9] Expanding on this definition, one can understand that imagination is essential in the creative process:

Imagination is the ability to form a mental image of something that is not perceived through the five senses. It is the ability of the mind to build mental scenes, objects or events that do not exist, are not present, or have happened in the past.... A developed and strong imagination does not make you a daydreamer and impractical. On the contrary, it strengthens your creative abilities, and is a great tool for recreating and remodeling your world and life... Imagination is a creative power that is necessary for inventing an instrument, designing a dress or a house, painting a picture or writing a book.[10]

What I love about this explanation is that the meaning of *chashab* includes many of the words already mentioned, like "to fabricate, to design, and to invent." In other words, if your heart is pure and you love the Lord, you will have no problem with your imagination because your imagination is sanctified. So, used your imagination to design, create, and invent marvelous works of art for the Lord. Let's look at Exodus 35:35 in the King James Version:

Them hath he filled with **wisdom of heart**, to work all manner of work, of the engraver, and of the cunning workman, and of the embroiderer, in blue, and in purple, in scarlet, and in fine linen, and of the weaver, even of them that do any work, and of those that devise cunning work.

I emphasize once again that it's the heart, the wisdom of the heart that makes the difference. But the word "maker," included in the meaning of several words related to art, rings a bell. Let's explore it.

GOD CREATOR AND MAKER

There are a variety of definitions for art. Art can be considered the creative activity or faculty of human beings through which they express ideas, emotions, values, or a vision of the world in particular. This is done using color, form, language, sound, and movement, which transform and combine to produce a unique work of art. Art can be, among other things, a song, a dance, a painting, or a play. Art is an aspect of culture, and many historians consider that it originated from a ritual or magical function and was transformed until it acquired an aesthetic component and a social function.

It is interesting to note that most ancient cultures did not know the concept of creativity and art was basically imitation. However, taking a look at the first verse in the first chapter of the Bible, we find the excellent manifestation of the Creation, resulting in the creative and artistic activity of the Creator: "In the beginning God created [*bara*] the heavens and the earth." *Bara*[11] is a Hebrew word that means "to create" from nothing (*ex nihilo*, Latin). If we employ the definition of it to the product that comes out of this first act of creation, one primarily sees a unique masterpiece. The heavens and earth did not exist before this moment. Both are full of colors and a diversity of materials and sounds, among other things, that express the vision of God for humanity. God created a world full of beauty, an aesthetic component, and He created it with a defined purpose.

And in the marvelous creative act of the human being, Creator God "breathed into his nostrils the breath of life, and man became a living being" (Genesis 2:7). Creator God imparted His Spirit when He formed man because, before creating him, He had already determined how he would be: "Let us make man in our image, after our likeness" (Genesis 1:26a). God was not creating a

62

mechanical robot. Upon concluding the human being masterpiece, the Spirit of God, who inspired the Genesis writer, gave testimony of God and said, "So God created man in His own image; in the image of God He created him; male and female He created them" (Genesis 1:27). I like the way another version says it: "So God created human beings, making them to be like himself. He created them male and female" (GNT). Therefore, creativity is part of the image of God in us. Maybe for that reason, one has this desire and ability to make things.

Concerning creation's purpose, the psalmist says, "The heavens declare the glory of God" (Psalm 19:1a). David talks about the firmament as evidence of the creative power of God. In other words, the heavens proclaim the splendor, greatness, and beauty of God. And David continues, saying, "And the firmament shows His handiwork" (Psalms 19:1b). The Hebrew word for "handiwork" is *ma'aseh*.[12] *Ma'aseh* is about "action, activity, art, product (especially a poem)." And it's the same word used when referring to the "work" of a skillful craftsman (Exodus 26:1), a jeweler (Exodus 28:11), and a perfumer (Exodus 30:25).

The Old Testament also calls us to celebrate the "work" of God. The psalmist was overwhelmed with the majesty of the Lord as he looked at God's "work" of creation:

> When I consider Your heavens,
> the work [*ma'aseh*] of Your fingers,
> the moon and the stars,
> which You have established. (Psalm 8:3)

Or:

> From before You have laid the foundation of the earth, and the heavens are the work [*ma'aseh*] of Your hands. (Psalm 102:25)

The Greek translation of the Hebrew word *ma'aseh* is *poiema*,[13] which means, "what is made; work; creation." This definition caught my attention because I remembered having seen this word previously related to the creative process. This took me to Ephesians 2:10: "For we are His workmanship, created in Christ

Jesus for good works, which God prepared beforehand, so that we should walk in them." If we take the biblical text and study it more closely, we will get a surprise: "For we are his workmanship." In Greek, the word "workmanship" is *poiema*, which means "a product, something made, masterpiece." And "created" is *ktid'zo* in Greek.[14] It means, "to create which applies only to God who alone can make what was 'not there before' (*ex nihilo*, out of nothing)." This connects with "In the beginning God created [*bara, ex nihilo*, out of nothing] the heavens and the earth." And Genesis 1:27 says, "So God created [*bara, ex nihilo*, out of nothing] man in His own image, in the image of God He created [*bara, ex nihilo*, out of nothing] him; male and female He created [*bara, ex nihilo*, out of nothing] them." In other words, "Because we are a *poiema*, created out of nothing in Christ Jesus unto good works, which God hath before ordained that we should walk in them." We are a *poiema*, and how beautifully this confirms Genesis 1:27: we are God's masterpiece! A masterpiece is "a work done with extraordinary skill, a work of outstanding artistry."[15] And because we are His creation and a reflection of His image, we are also, as we discussed in Chapter 3, *b'tselem Elohim*, a "little creator."

However, the word "poem" didn't always have the connotation that it has in our day. Emilio Lledó, author of the book *El Concepto "Poíesis" en la Filosofía Griega: (The Concept of "Poíesis" in Greek Philosophy):*

> How has it been possible that a concept that meant "doing" in its concrete and material sense, was gradually discharging this meaning, coming to acquire another opposite: sublimation, and in many cases the separation and repulsion of that same matter, in whose real handling did the word arise? At what time could such a turn be needed? To what extent this change is made in Greece and "*poíesis*" meant for the Greeks what it means to us today?[16]

It is in the works of Homer, the ancient Greek poet who lived around 800–701BC and to whom the epic poems *The Iliad* and *The Odyssey* are attributed to, where the first examples of the word *poiéo* or poetry appear to us.[17] In its beginnings, the word was identified as a verb and meant "to do, fabricate, edify."[18] Poetry was a physical activity, something done with the hands. This makes us understand that it refers to a material object. It was fabricating, building something from something else. In other words, it is the manufacture of a product, for example, making or fabricating a table from wood.

Immediately, this first definition brought to memory verses from the book of Genesis: "Let us make man..." (Genesis 1:26); "Then the Lord God formed [yatsar], man from the dust of the ground" (Genesis 2:7). And Genesis 2:22 says, "Then the rib which the Lord God had taken from man, He made into a woman." Yatsar[19] means "form, mold," and it is used to describe the creative activity of God. In this manner, when Paul writes, "we are God's poem," he was describing the way God created us. He made us with his own hands. God created a product, the man, from something else, the dust of the earth. And He created the woman from the man's rib. Again, we see something made from another product that already existed.

Hesiod, who lived around 750–650 BC and is known as the father of Greek didactic poetry, after Homer, used the word "poetry" in the context of "brought into existence" or "created."[20] Again, verses from Genesis start to resonate in my spirit: "So God created man in His own image; in the image of God He created him" (Genesis 1:27). But Genesis 2:7 brings more light upon the creative act and states, "Then the Lord God formed man from the dust of the ground and breathed into his nostrils the breath of life, and man became a living being."

This creative process is vital because it is true that God created us from the dust of the earth, and in turn, He is the creator of that "dust of the earth." God creates "ex nihilo," that is, from nothing, but that material created from nothing gives form to man. Maybe to form man from His hands, God created an object or a product, but in the moment that He breathed the breath of life, He converted him into a living being. Therefore, he brought him "to existence." That is how, little by little, we discover and go in depth into what "we are God's poem" means. Even during Homer's period, "poetry" was "put, place, position," like "put into place or position."[21] Consider Genesis 2:8, which says, "The Lord God planted a garden in the east, in Eden, and there He placed the man whom He had formed."

Heraclitus (540–470 BC), another Greek philosopher, used the verb as *poieîn*, or poetry, as "beginning," or "start." What is created starts to exist in the same moment as the act of creation. In turn, the verb started to be used to characterize an artistic activity. And with Herodotus, the sense of "to compose" and "artistic creation" appeared.[22]

As we have seen, the Greek language, like every language, is not a static one, and as it was developing, much of its words acquired broader meanings. As language develops, suffixes appear. These are letters that are added to the root of a word to form another. In this manner, we add the suffix -*sis* to *poeîn* to obtain *poíesis*. *Poíesis* is, then, "creation as such,"[23] an active process, and the object of that *poíesis* or creative action is the "*poiema*," or poem and poetry as the whole poetic work of the poet.

Therefore, the "poem" is the creative action of God and not only "a work" or a "product" or "something made." It is more than that. We are the object of God's creative action. God created a work of masterful creativity.

So, by the time the apostle Paul was born, approximately AD 5, in Tarsus, Cilicia, the word poem had evolved in what one understood nowadays. One can find evidence in the Scriptures that the apostle Paul spoke Greek:

> As Paul was being led to the entrance of the compound, he said to the commander in Greek, "May I have a word with you?"
>
> The commander replied, "So you know Greek, do you? Aren't you that Egyptian fanatic who started a rebellion some time ago and led four thousand assassins out into the wilderness?"
>
> Paul answered, "I am, in fact, a Jew from Tarsus, in Cilicia, a well-known city of southern Turkey where I was born. I beg you, sir, please give me a moment to speak to these people."

When the commander gave his permission, Paul stood on the steps and gestured with his hands for the people to listen. When the crowd quieted down, Paul addressed them in Aramaic and said:

"Ladies and gentlemen, fellow believers and elders—please listen to me as I offer my defense." (Now, when everyone realized he was speaking to them in their Judean Aramaic language, the crowd became all the more attentive.) (Acts:21:37– 22:2, TPT)

Therefore, when the apostle Paul used the word *poiema*, he understood the meaning and connotations. I understand that when the apostle Paul says, "We are God's poem," he is narrating in one word all of God's creative process. The apostle Paul not only spoke Greek, but he also read Greek literature. Remember, he was a highly educated man. And he must have read about the Greek poets since he mentioned them in his preaching: "'For in Him we live and move and have our being.' As some of your **own poets** have said, 'We are His offspring'" (Acts 17:28) (emphasis mine).

Another interesting detail: the sophists (fifth and fourth centuries BC) were dedicated to the study and criticism of the poets in Greece. Until then, the poem's structural form was characterized by meter, rhythm, and alliteration. Even more, it was understood that there was a supernatural element in it. This was a "gift of superior power, that transcends the limits of the human person and by which is completely absorbed."[24] The sophists realized a double change: in place of the supernatural appear the previously studied psychological suggestion and production by technique. Gorgias, a sophist, determined that poetry comes from *logos*. He mentions that the *logos*, the word, is the thing that moves, the thing that provokes happiness or sadness. We have seen how the concept of the poem has gone deeper, converting it into "creation by word."

In Romans 1:20, we also find the word "poem." In this case, it is plural: "The invisible things about Him—His eternal power and deity—have been clearly seen since the creation of the world and are understood by the things that are made, so that they are without excuse." The words "by the things that are made" are the

Greek word "poems." If we go back to Genesis 1, we repeatedly find the phrase "and God said." In Genesis 1:3, "God said, 'Let there be light,' and there was light." In Genesis 1:6,8: "Then God said, "Let there be an expanse in the midst of the waters, and let it separate the waters from the waters... God called the expanse Heaven. So, the evening and the morning were the second day." And this continued until all the universe was created. God created the world through the Word.

According to Lledó, the poet and philosopher Plato, in his work *The Banquet*, defines the idea of creation (*poíēsis*) as a creative activity,[25] and "this creative activity is a mode of wisdom."[26] To Plato, "Poetry, which is a general name signifying every cause whereby anything proceeds from that which is not, into that which is; so that the exercise of every inventive art is poetry, and all such artist poets."[27] In other words, "the idea of 'creation' (*poíēsis*) is something multiple, because in reality every cause that passes anything from non-being to being is creation, so that also the work done in all the arts are creations and the architects of these are all creators (*poiētai*, poets)." This creative process indicates the act of bringing into being what was not before; it is about "doing" something that did not previously exist.

This creative process indicates the creative act of "bringing to be what was not." It is a creative force or supreme action of God (*Poíesis Theou*). It's about "doing" something that previously did not exist. In line with Platon, poetry provoked the pass of not-being to be. Therefore, I understand that when the apostle Paul writes in Romans 1:20, "For the invisible things of him from the creation of the world are clearly seen, being understood by the things that are made, even his eternal power and Godhead; so that they are without excuse." The apostle Paul was pointing to a world that was created by the Word of God, by that supreme being, the not known God, called the Lord:

"For as I passed by and looked up at your objects of worship, I found an altar with this inscription: TO THE UNKNOWN GOD. Whom you therefore unknowingly worship, Him I proclaim to you. God who made the world and all things in it, being Lord of heaven and earth, does not live in temples made by hands" (Acts 17:23–24).

Recent versions of the Bible have translated Ephesians 2:10 in a more accurate way to reflect, indeed, that we are the artistic creation of God:

> For we are His workmanship [His own **master work, a work of art**], created in Christ Jesus [reborn from above— spiritually transformed, renewed, ready to be used] for good works, which God prepared [for us] beforehand [taking paths which He set], so that we would walk in them [living the good life which He prearranged and made ready for us]. (AMP)

> For we are God's **masterpiece**, created in the Messiah Jesus to perform good actions that God prepared long ago to be our way of life. (ISV)

> For we are his **creative work**, having been created in Christ Jesus for good works that God prepared beforehand so we can do them. (NET)

> We have become his **poetry**, a re-created people that will fulfill the destiny he has given each of us, for we are joined to Jesus, the Anointed One. Even before we were born, God planned in advance *our destiny* and the good works we would do *to fulfill it*! (TPT)

> For we are the product of His hand, *heaven's poetry etched on lives*, created in the Anointed, Jesus, to accomplish the good works God arranged long ago. (VOICE)

In summary, the evolution of the word "poem" not only describes the immediate aspect of creating, but it narrates the history of creation (universe and man), identifying the Lord, as Creator God, producer of two beautiful works of art. For the first, through His Word, He created the universe, and for the second, through His own hands, the human being. He is identified as *Poiesis Theou*, Creator God.

This called to my attention that great Greek thinkers needed centuries to discover and explain the creative process. It is not that God needed the Greeks to understand what it was that He did when Genesis says, "In the beginning, God created the heaven and the earth." It is that the Greeks needed centuries of studies, debate, and explanations to understand the creative process, the artistic process. No, art does not begin with ancient civilizations, nor with the Greeks, nor was its origin in rituals or magic. Art begins with Creator God. And it is that Creator God who told Moses that He put creativity and artistic abilities and techniques in Bezalel, Oholiab, and in all wise of heart for them to do the artistic work that He designed. And it had to be done to confirm to all that He had shown them (Exodus 25:9).

Even though from the exterior, the Tabernacle's design seemed simple, it would hold magnificent pieces that would represent all the beauty and splendor of the Lord. The parts were going to be made with costly materials, and at the same time, they would be beautiful pieces of art. An example of this is the Ark of the Testimony, made entirely of acacia wood and covered with pure gold inside and out. The cornice, rings, and rod were also covered in pure gold, and so were the two beautiful cherubs over it, made from a solid piece of pure gold. There was nothing added; it was one piece marvelously created. I imagine it had to be truly majestic because it would be the piece that went in the Holiest place, where God promised Moses, "I will meet with you there, and I will meet with you from above the mercy seat, from between the two cherubim which are upon the ark of the testimony. I will speak with you all that I will command you for the children of Israel" (Exodus 25:22).

BEYOND THE TABERNACLE

I understand that the artistic manifestations in the Scriptures are abundant. In a general look at art in the Bible, we find a diversity of artistic expressions. Let's look, for example, at a couple of them. Related to music, since the beginnings of humanity, we see the Bible provides testimony not only of music, but also of the confection of the musical instruments. It mentions that Jubal was the creator of musical instruments, instruments of string and wind: "Adah gave birth to Jabal... His brother's name was Jubal. He was the father of all those who play the harp and flute" (Genesis 4:20–21). And music was a vital part in the school of prophets:

> "After that you will come to the hill of God, where the garrison of the Philistines is. And when you come there to the city, you will meet a group of prophets coming down from the high place with a harp, a tambourine, a flute, and a lyre before them. And they will prophesy." (1 Samuel 10:5)

> "Now bring me a musician." And when the musician played, the hand of the Lord came upon him (2 Kings 3:15).

Another artistic manifestation we see from the first pages of the Bible is dance: "The prophet Miriam, Aaron's sister, took her tambourine, and all the women followed her, playing tambourines and dancing" (Exodus 15:20).

And perhaps one of the hidden treasures I've discovered is the use of art in education. During the Middle Ages, the ecclesiastical authorities started to use theater to teach biblical histories and their spiritual values to the people through religious dramas called mysteries. By the middle of the 20th century, an educational movement surged in the United States of America and in England; they understood that the arts could be an efficient educational instrument. Once again, a look at the Scriptures shows that the Lord already knew about it. God tells Moses, "Now therefore write yourself this song and teach it to the children of Israel. Put it on their mouths, so that this song may be a witness for Me against the children of Israel" (Deuteronomy 31:19). And the Scriptures state that Moses not only wrote the song, but he taught it to the children of Israel (Deuteronomy 31:22).

I wonder, why write a song specifically and teach it to the people? They already had the Ten Commandments, they had a series of laws, they had the Tabernacle, and above all, they had seen the wonders of God. Nevertheless, God understood something about art that maybe Moses did not know and that it took educators and artists centuries to comprehend: "Then when many disasters and troubles have fallen on them, this song will testify against them as a witness, for it must not be forgotten from the mouths of their descendants. For I know their intention which they are developing even now, before I have brought them into the land which I promised" (Deuteronomy 31:21). The phrase "this song will testify against them as a witness, for it must not be forgotten from the mouths of their descendants" means the song would not be quickly forgotten. In a time where Scripture was limited, there weren't books, recorders, CDs, or iPods. God knew that music was the most reliable way for people to remember what He had done for them. Furthermore, studies in the music and memory area confirm music better stimulates memory.

Definitively, Bezalel and his companions needed the gift of art; they needed that touch of excellence of the Spirit of God and artistic virtuosity that gave the artistic capacity so that all could be done for "honor and beauty" (Exodus 28:2, 40). *Poiesis Theou*, the Creator God from which creativity and art emanates, turned Bezalel into *b'zelem Elohim*, a small creator to do an extraordinary work of art. And that same Master Creator has called you by your name and has bestowed on you the gift of art.

NOTES:

[1] James Strong, LL., S. T. D., *The New Strong's Expanded Exhaustive Concordance of the Bible*, (Nashville: Thomas Nelson, 2010), 159.

[2] William Wilson, *Wilson's Old Testament Word Studies*, (Massachusetts: Hendrickson Publishers), 488.

[3] James Strong, LL., S. T. D., *The New Strong's Expanded Exhaustive Concordance of the Bible*, (Nashville: Thomas Nelson, 2010), 159.

[4] William Wilson, *Wilson's Old Testament Word Studies*, (Massachusetts: Hendrickson Publishers), 488.

[5] Finis Jennings Dake, *Dake's Annotated Reference Bible*, (Georgia, Dake Publishing, Inc., 2014), 193.

[6] James Strong, LL., S. T. D., *The New Strong's Expanded Exhaustive Concordance of the Bible*, (Nashville: Thomas Nelson, 2010), 100.

[7] _____, *The New Strong's Expanded Exhaustive Concordance of the Bible*, (Nashville: Thomas Nelson, 2010), 267.

[8] _____, *The New Strong's Expanded Exhaustive Concordance of the Bible*, (Nashville: Thomas Nelson, 2010), 100.

[9] https://www.yourdictionary.com/imagination.

[10] https://www.successconsciousness.com/index_000007.htm.

[11] James Strong, LL., S. T. D, *The New Strong's Expanded Exhaustive Concordance of the Bible*, (Nashville: Thomas Nelson, 2010), 45.

[12] _____, *The New Strong's Expanded Exhaustive Concordance of the Bible*, (Nashville: Thomas Nelson, 2010), 166.

[13] _____, *The New Strong's Expanded Exhaustive Concordance of the Bible*, (Nashville: Thomas Nelson, 2010), 205.

[14] _____, *The New Strong's Expanded Exhaustive Concordance of the Bible*, (Nashville: Thomas Nelson, 2010), 146.

[15] https://www.merriam-webster.com/dictionary/masterpiece.

[16] Emilio Lledó, *El concepto "poíesis" en la filosofía griega*, (Madrid: Edición de Alfonso Silva, 2010 0, 15–16.

[17] _____, *El concepto "poíesis" en la filosofía griega*, (Madrid: Edición de Alfonso Silva, 2010 0, 154.

[18] _____, *El concepto "poíesis" en la filosofía griega*, (Madrid: Edición de Alfonso Silva, 2010), 19.

[19] James Strong, LL., S. T. D., *The New Strong's Expanded Exhaustive Concordance of the Bible*, (Nashville: Thomas Nelson, 2010), 118.

[20] Emilio Lledó, *El concepto "poíesis" en la filosofía griega*, (Madrid: Edición de Alfonso Silva, 2010), 18.

[21] _____, *El concepto "poíesis" en la filosofía griega*, (Madrid: Edición de Alfonso Silva, 2010), 20.

[22] _____, *El concepto "poíesis" en la filosofía griega*, (Madrid: Edición de Alfonso Silva, 2010), 154.

[23] _____, *El concepto "poíesis" en la filosofía griega*, (Madrid: Edición de Alfonso Silva, 2010), 38.

[24] _____, *El concepto "poíesis" en la filosofía griega*, (Madrid: Edición de Alfonso Silva, 2010), 44.

[25] _____, *El concepto "poíesis" en la filosofía griega*, (Madrid: Edición de Alfonso Silva, 2010), 77.

[26] _____, *El concepto "poíesis" en la filosofía griega*, (Madrid: Edición de Alfonso Silva, 2010), 77.

[27] Plato, Shelley, Percy Bysshe, 1792–1822, 1870–1957, *The Banquet of Plato* (Chicago: Way and Williams, 1895), 90.

CHAPTER 6

ABILITY TO TEACH
A Creative Legacy

> I have filled him with the Spirit of God
> in wisdom, in understanding, in knowledge,
> and in all manner of craftsmanship.
> (Exodus 31:3)

> He also has put in his heart to teach.
> (Exodus 35:34a)

TEACHING OTHERS

Can you imagine teaching as part of the artistic call? How many of us dream of developing a career in which devote ourselves to do only our artistic work so we don't have to teach at all? I hear these complaints all the time from my fellow artists. However, by exploring Bezalel's call, I found teaching was one of the gifts that the Lord gave Bezalel. He was empowered by God "to teach" others the artistic skills necessary for the construction of the Tabernacle. Therefore, teaching is part of God's plan for the artist.

The Hebrew word "to teach" is *Yarah*, and it means "to throw, cast, direct, teach, instruct, point out, show."[1, 2] The word appears around 80 times in the Hebrew Old Testament.[3] It is interesting to see the evolution of the word. The first time the word *"Yarah"* appears is in Genesis 31:51: "Then Laban said to Jacob, 'See this pile and see this pillar which I have thrown [Yarah] between you and me.'" The word is also found in Exodus 15:4: "Pharaoh's chariots and his army He has thrown [Yarah] into the sea." According to Vine, the basic meaning of "to throw or cast" is seen in Joshua 18:6: "So describe the land in seven portions and return to me. Then I will cast [Yarah] lots for you here before the Lord our God." It is also seen in Exodus 15:4, when Pharaoh's chariots are thrown into the sea. From there, the idea of "to throw" is extended in two directions. First, it means the shooting of arrows, as in 1 Samuel 20:36: "And he said to his boy, 'Run, find the arrows which I shoot [*Yarah*].' He ran, and he shot [*Yarah*] the arrow over him." Second, it means "to point," as fingers are thrown in a certain direction, as in Genesis 46:28: "Now he sent Judah before him to Joseph, **to point out** the way before him to Goshen; and they came into the land of Goshen" (NASB, emphasis added). And from this second meaning, the concept of teaching evolved as the "pointing out" of facts and truth.[4]

In 4:12, the Lord says to Moses, "Now therefore go, and I will be with your mouth and teach you what you must say." I see a spiritual principle here, especially for those moments when you have to do something that God is asking but you have no idea how to do it. This principle would help Bezalel in his mission. God himself tells Moses that He will teach him what he must say. And in verse 15, He once again confirms that He will teach Moses what he must do: "You shall speak to him and put the words in his mouth, and I will be with your mouth, and with his mouth, **and will teach you what you must do**" (emphasis added).

This was something new for Moses. God was calling him to go back to Egypt to free the people. Moses was full of excuses: "O my Lord, I am not eloquent, neither before nor since You have spoken to Your servant. But I am slow of speech, and of a slow tongue." But God had a different point of view: "Who has made man's mouth? Or who made the dumb, or deaf, or the seeing, or the blind? Have not I, the Lord? Now therefore go, and I will be with your mouth and teach you what you must say."

After successfully freeing the people from Egypt, Moses needed to teach the people God's laws. In Exodus 18:20, God tells Moses what he needs to teach: "And you shall teach them the statutes and laws and shall show them the way in which they must walk and the work that they must do." In Exodus 24:12, the Lord invites Moses to meet with Him: "Come up to Me to the mountain and stay there, and I will give you the stone tablets with law and the commandments which I have written, so that you may teach them." God gave Moses the information; He gave Moses what he needed to teach.

I don't know exactly what Bezalel thought when he heard Moses saying, "He also has put in his heart to teach." It is interesting to note that in Exodus 31, the gift of teaching is not there. But when Moses told the children of Israel about Bezalel and Oholiab's calling, he said, "He also has put in his heart to teach, both he and Oholiab." I have no doubt that that was God's intention from the very beginning. Therefore, in the perfect plan of God, He starts by teaching and empowering us first. Then He tells us, "Now, you go and teach others."

I find in the Bible that it was the responsibility of the nation's leaders to teach. They set up the education system. Sometimes we want to do everything ourselves, but God has a better idea. For example, Exodus 18:17–20 says:

> Moses' father-in-law said to him, "What you are doing is not good.
>
> You will surely wear yourself out, both you, and these people who are with you, for this thing is too heavy for you. You are not able to do it by yourself.
>
> Now listen to me, I will advise you, and may God be with you: You be a representative for the people to God so that you may bring *their* disputes to God.

And you shall **teach** them the statutes and laws and shall **show** them the way in which they must walk and the work that they must do." (emphasis added)

And in 2 Chronicles 17:7–9, one can find:

In the third year of his reign he sent officials, Ben-Hail, Obadiah, Zechariah, Nethanel, and Micaiah, **to teach** in the cities of Jerusalem,

and with them were also the Levites: Shemaiah, Nethaniah, Zebadiah, Asahel, Shemiramoth, Jehonathan, Adonijah, Tobijah, and Tob-Adonijah, who were Levites. And with these were also Elishama and Jehoram, who were priests.

They **taught** *the people* in Judah, and they used the Book of the Law of the Lord and they traveled about all the cities of Judah and taught the people. (emphasis added)

In both Exodus 18:17–23 and 2 Chronicles 17:7–9, the nation's leader and his representatives set up the education system. So, it is not a surprise that once Bezalel became the director of the construction of the Tabernacle and Oholiab, his assistant, God gave them the gift of teaching. They were empowered and taught by God to make the Tabernacle. Now Bezalel and Oholiab need to impart to others what they had learned.

Merriam-Webster Dictionary defines "teach" as "any manner of imparting information or skill so that others may learn."[5] I find in the word *Yarah* different ways of teaching. For example, let's look again at the meanings of the word. *Yarah* means to throw, cast, direct, teach, instruct, point out, and show, among other things. As leaders, and especially as artists, Bezalel and Oholiab were going to need different ways of teaching. Let's explore the word "direct." According to the dictionary, "to direct" is "to carry out the organizing, energizing, and supervising of a project."[6] This was exactly what Bezalel was going to do. He was going to direct the construction of the Tabernacle, and he needed to organize the teams and prioritize the tasks. He also needed to keep everyone motivated, committed to the project, and in high spirits. The working conditions in the desert were probably not the best, and they were doing something that had no precedent. They were learning and doing it at the same time. Everything had to be done according to God's design. That was a huge challenge. Bezalel also needed to supervise the work because he had to present it before Moses for its approval. Consequently, implicit in the gift of teaching is the capacity to organize and supervise a project and encourage the people who work in it.

Yarah also means to show or demonstrate, and it "implies showing by action."[7] Let's look at the preparation of colors. One can explain how to do it or have someone read about it, but showing or demonstrating the process is a faster and more accurate way of teaching the skill. To instruct is "to give knowledge, to provide with authoritative information or advice, also implying greater explicitness or formality."[8] To direct and instruct "both connote expectation of obedience and usually concern specific points of procedure or method."[9] On the other hand, "to inform," another of the meanings of *Yarah*, "means to make one aware of something and implies the imparting of knowledge especially of facts or occurrences."[10] It's a less formal approach. And "to point out" means "to direct someone's attention to (someone or something) by pointing or to talk about or mention (something that one thinks is important)."[11] This can be useful when you want to highlight a specific point or detail.

It seems unexpected that Bezalel and Oholiab received the gift of teaching from the Lord. And this gift, even though it's mentioned last, is just as important as the first five. This gift capacitated them and prepared them to do the job in an organized way; at the same time, it helped them leave a powerful continuity and legacy for their nation. There would be moments to direct the project, and there would be moments to impart knowledge. Bezalel needed to know how to direct this project in such a way that it was in line with the design that the Lord had shown Moses. Sometimes the teaching needed to be given in a formal and structured manner, for example, the measures or the materials to be used and in what specific places or for which specific piece of furniture they would be used. And in other instances, they needed to demonstrate the procedure, for example, how to color the fabrics or skins to look the same all the time. I am sure there were demonstrations of how to weave, paint fabrics, cut wood, or melt metals.

Teaching is important. It is not only repeating information that has been memorized, though memorization is important. For example, the Lord told Moses, "Now therefore write yourself this song and teach it to the children of Israel. Put it on their mouths, so that this song may be a witness for Me against the children of Israel" (Deuteronomy 31:19). The children of Israel needed to memorize the song. At the same time, there are things that you can teach by telling a story, while others are learned just by being around the teacher and listening.

In Romans 12, the apostle Paul wrote about a series of gifts the Lord gives to His people, and one of them is teaching. Also, in Ephesians 4:11, there is a description of the five-fold ministry, and among them are teachers. Verse 12 tells us the purpose of the five-fold ministry: "for the equipping of the saints, for the work of service, and for the building up of the body of Christ." I strongly believe that from the very beginning of time, God wanted us to share our gift of art with others, and what better way to do it than through teaching?

On the other hand, if there are teachers, there are students. As students, we need to be humble and recognize when to ask for help. One way to grow is to register in a workshop or go back to school for more intense training. It is necessary to know the technique of how to work the artistic medium in which you have ability. I understand God gives the gift of teaching because learning is important and necessary. There can't be teachers without students. Sometimes we are quick to judge the people who study. Nevertheless, God gave the gift of teaching to Bezalel and Oholiab. I understand that some people may receive the gift of art in a supernatural way; others need to be taught. The important thing is to use your gift to glorify God, and there is always space to grow.

If God called you to sing, study singing, and if He called you to dance, study dance. You can start to develop the talent slowly; we all have a beginning. Either way, I understand studying is important to develop talent. I have known people who say, "I don't study because the Lord gave me talent." Perfect. God gave you talent, and with talent comes the responsibility to develop it. If it is true that God gave you the talent and you don't need to develop it because He gave it to you completely developed, we will all be a witness to it and rejoice, and God will be glorified through it. But when I look at what you have to offer and see that the artistic manifestation lacks a level of excellence, I ask myself, "What happened?"

To clarify the point of studying, I am not only talking about university programs. You can take classes with independent teachers, or at church, community workshops, or art institutes, among other places. You can start with a single class or as an apprentice in a group. The idea is that the gift that God deposited in you gets developed so you can take it to a level of excellence where even the ones who don't know God can say, like Pharaoh when Joseph interpreted his dreams, "Can we find anyone like this man, in whom is the Spirit of God?" (Genesis 41:38).

Bezalel and Oholiab got six gifts, and among them was the gift of teaching. I am more than sure that there were people who wanted to participate in the construction of the Tabernacle and had the calling but maybe had no idea how to prepare the colors or how to cut wood, but Bezalel and Oholiab were ready to share their knowledge with them. As a result, they did everything according to what God commanded Moses, and the people who had the skills shared them with the one who didn't. Therefore, the Tabernacle was built with a high level of excellence, and the Lord was glorified.

NOTES:
[1] James Strong, LL.D., S.T.D., *The New Strong's Expanded Exhaustive Concordance of the Bible*, (Nashville: Thomas Nelson), 257.

[2] Robert Young, *Young's Analytical Concordance to the Bible*, (Peabody, MA: Hendrickson Publishers, 2011), 962.

[3] W. E. Vine, *Vine's Complete Expository Dictionary of Old and New Testament Words* (Nashville: Thomas Nelson), 120–121.

[4] _____. *Vine's Complete Expository Dictionary of Old and New Testament Words* (Nashville: Thomas Nelson), 257.

[5] https://www.merriam-webster.com/dictionary/teach.

[6] https://www.merriam-webster.com/dictionary/direct.

[7] https://www.merriam-webster.com/dictionary/show.

[8] https://www.merriam-webster.com/dictionary/direct.

[9] https://www.merriam-webster.com/dictionary/direct.

[10] https://www.merriam-webster.com/dictionary/inform.

[11] https://www.merriam-webster.com/dictionary/point%20out.

CONCLUSION

TOWARDS A
THEOLOGY OF ART

T he story of Bezalel still amazes me: an artist called by God. Even more, I still remember the moment when I discovered his story. After discovering Bezalel, I dreamed of God calling my name and setting me apart to be an artist. I dreamed of using art as an instrument of transformation for God's glory. I also continue to have an immense desire to see that in the same manner that God shows the design of the Tabernacle to Moses, He will do the same to us. And since then, I proposed in my heart to tell the story of Bezalel to every artist. This book is an extension of that dream. I wanted for you to discover Bezalel and especially that you, too, appropriate the six gifts that God gave Bezalel, Oholiab, and the group of wise-hearted artists who collaborated with Bezalel.

After I discovered Bezalel, I continued to conduct research into his artistic calling, the work of the Tabernacle, and his accomplishment. In the beginning, the information was limited, but I was hungry for God and for the arts. During the process, I had dreams and visions about God's plan for the arts. That kept me going. And I discovered a divine pattern. I called it the theology of art. Why did I call it this? I have a very simple answer. Theology comes from two Greek words: "Theos," which means God, and "logy," which comes from "logos" (word); therefore, theology is the study of God as He is revealed in the Bible, the Word of God. So, when I say theology of art, I am studying what God says in the Bible about art. I think the story of the calling of Bezalel includes the foundation or guidelines of a possible theology of art.

Bezalel is also a wonderful role model for contemporary artists. Probably, there were moments when Bezalel felt the desire to add his personal or particular touch to the Tabernacle. Nevertheless, the Bible says that Bezalel made everything "as the Lord commanded Moses." Bezalel made Moses look good before the Lord. And these are major words. The commandment that Moses received was unique. Remember that the Lord had convocated a reunion in the mountain that lasted forty days and forty nights. There, He gave the Ten Commandments to Moses, the general laws that would serve as a guideline to a nation that was barely forming, and He showed how the Tabernacle would be made. Bezalel's obedience made Moses look good before God. I can say Moses stood with his head held high before the Lord and, with great satisfaction, that all was made "as it was shown on the mountain."

The Tabernacle, in our day, is a testimony of the plan of salvation for our lives, a shadow of what was to come, JESUS. And the obedience of Bezalel made the Lord's message arrive intact. I understand that Bezalel is to us artists an example of obedience, submission, and character contrary to what happened, for instance, with Korah. We have seen how Bezalel successfully completed the task to which he was called and capacitated.

When I wanted to learn about art in the Bible, I asked God, and He directed my steps to Exodus 31 and 35, and there I met Bezalel, his calling, and his accomplishment. Through these passages, I found the biblical foundation of what I understand can be the theology of art.

Therefore, I envision a theology of art:

- That proclaims that art is God's will and a gift from the God Creator to humanity.
- That declares that artists are creators by divine nature and that in the moment of our creation, God

breathes His Spirit, giving us His breath of life,
imparting in us His Creator Spirit.

- That understands artists are chosen and called by
  name by the Lord.
- That announces that God fills artists with His Holy
  Spirit.
- That celebrates that God empowers artists with the
  spirit of wisdom.
- That states that God invests artists with the spirit of
  understanding.
- That pronounces that God has endowed artists with
  the spirit of knowledge.
- That rejoices that God has enabled artists with the
  spirit of art and creativity.
- That delights that God has inspired artists with the
  ability to teach.
- That makes known that God loves for artists to obey
  and submit to God and leaders.
- That acknowledges that artists are under the
  shadow and special protection of the Most-High
  God.
- That understands that artists are a shadow born
  from the light of the Creator.
- That knows that artists are the reflection of the
  Creator God, small creators.
- That encourages artists to recognize God and His
  Word as their light.
- That teaches artists that their lives must be
  completely dedicated to God.
- That recognizes that artists are worshipers, that we
  belong to the tribe of Judah (praise), called to
  emphasize the glory of God.
- That teaches artists to reflect the greatness of our
  God.

- That knows that only the artist who loves God and respects His laws can fulfill the commitment to create art for the glory of God.
- That recognizes that artistic talent is not limited to the Church alone. God has given it to us for the blessing of humanity, for "glory and honor" of his name. And if we only glorify God in the Church, how will we enlighten the secular world that does not know Him? In the same way that rulers and peoples saw God through the work developed by Joseph, Solomon, and Daniel, humanity can see and glorify God through our artistic work.

I understand that as artists called by God, we need to shine and reflect His glory. And it is in this moment when, as artists, Jesus is telling us, "You are the light of the world. A city that is set on a hill cannot be hidden. Neither do men light a candle and put it under a basket, but on a candlestick. And it gives light to all who are in the house. Let your light so shine before men that they may see your good works and glorify your Father who is in heaven" (Mathew 5:14–16).

APPENDICES

APPENDIX A
The Work to Complete

According to the order of appearance in the Bible, from Exodus 25 to Exodus 30, God commands Moses to do the following:

THE ARK OF THE COVENANT

Exodus 25:10–22

Measurements

- Length 3.67 feet (1.12 meters)
- Width 2.23 feet (68 centimeters)
- Height 2.23 feet (68 centimeters)

Specifications:

- The ark will be made of acacia wood.
- It will be covered inside and out with pure gold.
- It shall have a gold border round it.
- It will have gold rings in the four corners. Two rings shall be in the one side of it, and two rings in the other side of it, for a total of four rings of pure gold.
- It will have poles of acacia wood overlaid with gold.
- The poles will be put into the rings by the sides of the ark so that the ark may be borne with them, and they will be kept on the rings of the ark all the time.

Purpose:

- "You shall put into the ark the testimony which I shall give you." (Exodus 25:16). Hebrews 9:4 says, "which contained the golden censer and the ark of the covenant overlaid with gold, containing the golden pot holding the mana, Aaron's rod that budded, and the tablets of the covenant." (The tables of the covenant are the Ten Commandments, Deuteronomy 10:1–5).

MERCY SEAT

Measurements:

- Length 3.67 feet (1.12 meters)
- Width 2.23 feet (68 centimeters)
- It is the mercy seat (the top of the ark), made of pure gold.
- The mercy seat, along with the two cherubim at its extremities, will be made from one single piece of material.
- The mercy seat will go on top of the Ark of the Covenant in the Most Holy (Exodus 26:34).

Purpose:

- "I will meet with you there, and I will meet with you from above the mercy seat, from between the two cherubim which are upon the ark of the testimony. I will speak with you all that I will command you for the children of Israel" (Exodus 25:22).

THE CHERUBIM

Specifications:

- Made from gold wrought by a hammer.
- One cherub at one end, and the other cherub at the other end. The cover and the cherubim at both extremes will be made from one single piece of material.
- The wings of the two cherubs will extend upwards in such a manner that they will cover the top of the ark, and they will be one in front of the other. The faces of the cherubim will look towards the mercy seat.

FURNITURE AND ACCESSORIES

The Table for the Showbread (Bread of the Proposition)

Exodus 25:23–30

Measurements:

- Length 3 feet (90 centimeters).
- Width 1.5 feet (45 centimeters).
- Height 2.23 feet (68 centimeters).

Specifications:

- Table made from acacia wood overlaid with pure gold.
- It will have a gold border around it.
- It will have four rings of gold, which will be at the four corners.
- Over against the border, shall the rings be for the staves to bear the table.
- Two rods of acacia wood, overlaid with gold, that the table may be carried with them.
- The dishes, spoons, pitchers, and bowls with which to pour drink offerings will be of pure gold.
- The table will be outside of the veil, at the north side (Exodus 26:35).

Purpose:

- "You shall set the showbread on the table before Me always" (Exodus 25:30).

The Gold Lampstand (Candlestick of Gold)

Exodus 25:31–39

Measurements:

- The lampstand, with all its utensils, will be made of 75 pounds (34 kilos) of pure gold. Some researchers calculate the weight was around 107 pounds since the exact weight of a gold talent is unknown.

Specifications:

- The lampstand, its foot or base, and cane will be wrought by hammer.
- From its sides will come six branches, three branches from one side of the candlestick and three from the other side of the candlestick.
- There will be three cups in the form of almond flowers in one arm, with an apple and a flower, and three cups in the form of almond flowers in the other arm, with an apple and a flower.
- In the cane of the candlestick shall be four bowls made like unto almond flowers, with their knops or apples and their flowers.
- There shall be an apple under the first two branches of it, and an apple under the next two branches of it, and an apple under the last two branches of it, according to the six branches that proceed out of the candlestick.
- Its apple and its branches shall be of one single piece of material.
- All shall be one beaten work of pure gold.
- Seven lamps, the tongs thereof, and the snuff dishes shall be of pure gold.
- The candlestick will be in front of the table at the side of the Tabernacle to the south (Exodus 26:35).

Purpose:

- "You shall make its seven lamps, and they shall light its lamp so that they may give light to the area in front of it" (Exodus 25:37).

THE TABERNACLE

The Curtains of Twined Linen

Exodus 26:1–6

Measurements:

- The length of each curtain will be 42 feet (12.6 meters).
- The width of each curtain will be six feet (1.8 meters).
- All the curtains will have the same measurements.

Specifications:

- The tabernacle will have 10 curtains of twined linen of blue (a mixture of indigo and dark red), purple, and scarlet, with cherubims of cunning work.
- Five of the curtains will be coupled one with the other. Also, the other five curtains will be coupled one with the other.
- Bows in blue fabric on the edge of one of the curtains of the extreme of the first selvage in the coupling; and likewise, in the uttermost edge of another curtain, in the coupling of the second.
- 50 bows in one curtain and 50 bows in the edge of the curtain that is in the coupling of the second, that the loops may take hold one of another.
- 50 taches of gold and couple the curtains together with the taches so it will be one unit.

The Curtains of Goat Hair

Exodus 26:7–13

Measurements:

- Eleven curtains of the same measurements.
- The length of each curtain will be 45 feet (13.5 meters).
- The width of each curtain will be 6 feet (1.8 meters).

Specifications:

- The curtains of goat's hair to be a covering upon the tabernacle.

- Five curtains coupled by themselves, and six curtains by themselves.
- The sixth curtain will be doubled in the forefront of the tabernacle.
- Fifty bows on the edge of one curtain that is outmost in the coupling, and 50 bows in the edge of the curtain which coupleth the second.
- Fifty taches of brass. The taches will be put into the bows to couple the tent together that it may be one.
- The remnant that remains of the curtains of the tent, the half curtain that remains, shall hang over the backside of the tabernacle.
    o On one side, 1.5 feet (45 centimeters).
    o On the other side, 1.5 feet (45 centimeters) of what remains of the length of the tent curtains.
    o It shall hang over the sides of the tabernacle on one side and on the other to cover it.

Purpose: Cover for the Tabernacle's roof.

A Cover of Rams' Skins

Exodus 26:14a

Specifications:

- Rams' skins dyed red.

Purpose:

- To weatherproof the tent.

A Cover of Porpoise Skins

Exodus 26:14b

Specifications:

- Cover for the tent.

Purpose:

- To weatherproof the tent.

THE TABERNACLE STRUCTURE

Exodus 26:15–37

The Vertical Boards

Exodus 26:15–25

Measurements:

- Length of each board: 15 feet (4.5 meters)
- Width of each board: 2 feet (68 meters)

Specifications:

- The vertical boards for the tabernacle will be of acacia wood and will be put vertically.
- Each board will have two tenons to unite with each other.
- 20 boards to the south side.
- 40 sockets of silver under the 20 boards: two sockets under one board for its two tenons and two sockets under another board for its two tenons.
- For the second side of the tabernacle, on the north side, 20 boards and its 40 sockets of silver: two sockets under one board, and two sockets under another board.
- For the sides of the tabernacle, westward, six boards. Two boards for the corners of the tabernacle in the posterior part.
- They will be double underneath, coupled together above the head of it unto one ring.
- This will be for both of them: they will form the two corners. There will be 16 boards with silver sockets: two sockets under one board, and two sockets for the other.

Bars of Acacia Wood

Exodus 26:26–30

Specifications:

- Five bars of acacia for the boards of one side of the tabernacle.

- Five bars for the boards of the other side of the tabernacle, and five bars for the boards of the side of the tabernacle, for the two sides westward.
- The middle bar in the center of the boards will go from one end to another.
- The boards will be overlaid with gold, and the rings will be of gold where the bars will be placed. The bars will be overlaid with gold.
  Note: The vital function of the boards was to strengthen the structure of the Tabernacle by uniting the boards and maintaining them firmly together.

Purpose:

- "And thou shalt rear up the tabernacle according to the fashion thereof which was shewed thee in the mount" (Exodus 26:30).

The Veil

Exodus 26:31–33

Specifications:

- Veil of blue fabric, and purple, and scarlet, and fine twined linen. It will be made with cherubs of cunning work.
- It will hang upon four pillars of acacia wood overlaid with gold.
- Their hooks shall be of gold, upon four sockets of silver.
- The veil will hang under the taches, and behind the veil will be the Ark of the Testimony.
- The veil, 30 feet from the Tabernacle's aperture.

Purpose:

- The veil shall divide the holy place and the most holy.

Tabernacle's Door

Exodus 26:36–37

Specifications:

- Of blue, purple, and scarlet fabric, and fine twined linen, wrought with needlework.
- Five pillars of acacia wood for the curtain overlaid with gold.
- The hooks will be of gold, too.
- Five sockets will be cast of brass for them.

Purpose:

- A curtain for the tent's entrance.

THE ATRIUM AND THE DOOR

Exodus 27:9–19
   The Atrium

   Exodus 27:9–19

Measurements and Specifications:

- To the south side will be curtains of twined linen for the atrium, of 150 feet (45 meters) of length for one side.
- Its pillars will be 20, with its 20 sockets of brass.
- The hooks of the pillars and moldings will be of silver.
- Likewise, for the north side, there shall be curtains of (150 feet) 45 meters in length and its 20 pillars and 20 sockets of brass.
- The hooks of the pillars and their fillets will be of silver.
- And for the width of the court/atrium on the west side shall be curtains of 75 feet (22.5 meters) with its ten pillars and ten sockets.
- And the width of the court/atrium on the east side will 75 feet.
- The curtains of one side of the gate shall be 22.5 feet (6.75 meters) with three pillars and three sockets.
- For the other side, there will be curtains of 22.5 feet (6.75 meters) with three pillars and three sockets.

- The door of the court/atrium, there will be a curtain of 30 feet (9 meters) of blue fabric, purple, and scarlet, and fine twined linen, wrought with needlework: and their pillars shall be four, and their sockets four.
- All the pillars round about the court shall have silver moldings; their hooks shall be of silver, and their sockets of brass.
- The length of the court/atrium will be 150 feet (45 meters), the width 75 feet (22.5 meters) by each side, and height of 7.5 feet (2.25 meters); its curtain of fine twined linen, and their sockets of brass.
- All the vessels of the tabernacle in all the service, all the pins, and all the pins of the court/atrium shall be of brass.

Atrium's Door

Exodus 27:16

Specifications:

- For the atrium's door, there will be a curtain of 30 feet (9 meters).
- Blue fabric, purple, and scarlet, and fine twined linen, of needlework.
- Four pillars with its four sockets.

The Bronze Altar

Exodus 27:1–8

Specifications:

- Altar of acacia wood.
- 7.5 feet of length (2.25 meters).
- 7.5 feet of width (2.25 meters), the altar will be square.
- 4.5 feet of height (1.35 meters).
- Horns in its four corners.
- The horns shall be of the same piece of the altar, overlaid with brass.

- Make pans to receive the ashes, shovels, basins, meat hooks, and firepans.
- All the vessels will be made of bronze.
- Grill of brass made as a net; and upon the net, four bronze rings in the four corners, under the altar's border, so the net reaches up to the middle of the altar.
- Bars for the altar, bars of acacia, overlaid in bronze.
- The bars shall be put into the rings so they will be on the two sides of the altar when it's transported.
- Hollow with boards, as it was shown on the mountain.

SACRED WARDROBE

Exodus 28:1–4

Specifications:

- Materials: gold, blue fabric, purple, scarlet, and fine linen.
- Holy wardrobe for Aaron.
- Wardrobe: a vest, ephod, mantle, tunic stitched in squares, a tiara, and a belt.

Purpose:

- For glory and beauty.
- To consecrate Aaron and his sons as priests.

Ephod of Gold

Exodus 28:6–7

Specifications:

- Of blue fabric, purple, and scarlet, and fine twined linen, with cunning work.
- It will have two shoulder pieces that will be joined at the two edges so they can be joined together.
- Two onyx stones, with the names of the 12 sons of Israel engraved in them.

- Six of the names in one stone and six other names on the other stone, all in order by birthday.
- Two chains of pure gold, in the form of braided laces, fastened to the ouches.

The Belt

Specifications:

- Cunning needlework, over the ephod.
- Material: gold, blue fabric, purple, scarlet and of fine twined linen.

The Vest

Exodus 28:15–21

Specifications:

- Of cunning work
- Similar to the ephod materials: gold, blue fabric, purple, and scarlet, and fine twined linen.
- Square and double, 9 inches (25 cm)
- It will have four lines of stones
  - The first line will consist of a sardius, a topaz, and a carbuncle (emerald).
  - The second row shall be an emerald, a sapphire, and a diamond.
  - The third row a ligure, an agate, and an amethyst.
  - The fourth row a beryl, an onyx, and a jasper.
  - They shall be set in gold in their inclosings.
  - There will be 12 stones, as the names of the sons of Israel.
  - Like the engravings of a signet, everyone with his name shall they be according to the 12 tribes.

The Mantle of the Ephod

Exodus 28:31–35

Specifications:

- The mantle of the ephod was all in blue fabric.
- There will be an opening in the middle of its superior part.
- It shall have a binding of woven work around the opening, as it were the hole of a habergeon, that it be not rent.
- Beneath upon the hem of it, it will have pomegranates of blue, and of purple, and of scarlet, round about the hem; and bells of gold between them round about: a golden bell and a pomegranate, another golden bell and another pomegranate upon the hem of the robe round about.

Purpose:

- It shall be upon Aaron to minister.
- Its sound shall be heard when he goes into the holy place before the Lord, and when he comes out, so he does not die.

Plate of Pure Gold

Exodus 28:36–38

Specifications:

- Plate of pure gold.
- Engraved, like the engravings of a signet, HOLINESS TO THE LORD.
- It will be put on a blue lace that it may be upon the tiara; in the front.

Purpose:

- The plate will always be in front of Aaron so he obtains grace before Jehovah.

TUNICS, MITER, BELTS, TIARAS, AND UNDERPANTS

Exodus 28:39–43

Specifications:

- Embroidered coat/tunic of fine linen.
- A mitre or tiara of fine linen.

- A girdle/belt of needlework.
- Coats/tunics, girdle/belt, and bonnets or tiaras for Aaron's sons.
- Linen underwear from the loins to the thighs.

ALTAR TO BURN THE INCENSE, PILE OF BRASS, ANOINTING OIL, AND THE INCENSE

Altar to burn the incense

Exodus 30:1–10

Measurements:

- Square: 18 square inches (45 cm)
- 3 feet (90 cm) of height

Specifications:

- Made from acacia wood.
- The horns shall be of the same piece.
- Overlaid with pure gold: the top, the sides, and the horns.
- It will have a crown of gold round about.
- Two golden rings under the crown of it, by the two corners, upon the two sides, and they shall be to place the bars and be transported.
- Bars of acacia wood and overlaid with gold.
- Altar position: in front of the veil that is by the ark of the testimony, before the mercy seat that is over the testimony.

Purpose:

- Aaron shall burn sweet incense every morning upon it when he prepares the lamps.

Metal Fountain

Exodus 30:17–21

Specifications:

- Metal base (brass).

- Placed between the tabernacle of the congregation and the altar, with water in it.

Purpose:

- To wash. With it, Aaron and his sons shall wash their hands and their feet upon entering the tent of the testimony so they do not die.
- Also, when they come near to the altar to minister, to burn offerings made by fire unto the LORD: they will wash their hands and their feet so they do not die.
- It shall be a statute forever to them.

The Oil of Anointing

Exodus 30:22–33

Specifications:

Take from the finest spices:

- Pure Myrrh, 18 pounds
    - Sweet cinnamon, half, 9 pounds
    - Sweet calamus, 9 pounds
    - Sweet cassia, 18 pounds
    - Olive oil, 1.5 gallons
- Mix

Purpose:

- It will be oil for the holy anointing
- To anoint:
    - The tent of reunion
    - The Ark of the Pact
    - The table and all its utensils
    - The candlestick and all its utensils
    - The altar of incense
    - The altar of holocaust and all its utensils
    - The pile and its base
    - Aaron and his sons

The Incense

Exodus 30:34–38

Specifications:

- Sweet spices, stacte, onycha (tree resin), galbanum (originally, it was obtained from a plant that produces a milky substance of rubbery consistency), and clean incense (aromatic resin and rubbery), each one of the same weight or quantity (ratio/equal parts).
- With it, a perfume will be made (incense), a confection after the art of the apothecary, tempered together, pure, and holy.
- Some of it shall be beaten very finely. A part of it will be put before the testimony in the tabernacle of testimony/congregation.
- This incense won't be made in the same proportions for proper or personal use because this proportion is specific, consecrated to Jehovah.

Purpose:

- The incense will be holy for Jehovah. Whosoever makes an incense like this to use it as perfume will be cut off from his people.

APPENDIX B
ART IN THE PROPHETIC PLAN OF GOD

Months after learning about the calling of Bezaleel and after accepting God's invitation in my own life, I had a vision. I saw two gear wheels, two golden wheels. Each wheel was the same as the other one. In my spirit, I asked what the meaning of what I was seeing was, and a voice within my spirit started to explain that one wheel represented the people that God was calling and separating for the events of the end times. "Every thread represents a person," the voice said. And I saw in my spirit how a huge hand would pull people from different places and put them together to build the wheel. He emphasized that every thread had to be identical to the others: "No one was more important than the other." Then He said, "The second wheel represents my Word, and when the two wheels engage together, they will roll along perfectly."

The reason why each thread has to be the same size, the voice explained to me, is that when the wheels engage together, each thread should fit exactly into the space of the other wheel, like a puzzle, so that when they engage, they can roll softly and within each other. "If one thread is larger than the other, the wheels will not be able to engage together. Thus, they will not move," He said. In my vision, when the two wheels engaged and started to roll, streams of water came out from the union. "The water," the voice of my spirit continuously said to me, "is the Holy Spirit covering the earth." And the instrument that God was using so that this could happen was art; I saw the water falling upon Puerto Rico and down unto Central and South America and the rest of the world.

Then I heard the voice again speaking to my spirit and telling me that the time would come when we would see different places and even countries closed to the preaching of the Word in all traditional ways, but that there would be artists from different parts of the world who were prepared by God and capable of spreading the message of salvation through art. And I understand that like Esther, we have been called for this time.

APPENDIX C
LIZETTE AYALA LETTER (1980)

June 19th, 1980

Bretton Hall College of the Arts
West Bretton, "New Wakefield"
West Yorkshire, England

Alma,

[...] Look, Rafael invited Mayra and me to talk about our experiences in Christian theater at a youth assembly. I was going to tell him no at first, but the truth is I have never had the experience to testify on that particular subject or to support him, not only biblically but as a way to create conscience and impact the non-believer. When I was preparing to talk about theater, I wanted to bring Bible verses that sustained my position. And do you know what, Alma? You should remember something you told me once and I never forgot. I am referring to the Bible verse of Exodus 31 that narrates God's calling to two men, Bezaleel and Aholiab, and how God told them through Moses and before the children of Israel that He had filled them of

1. Spirit of God
2. Wisdom
3. Intelligence
4. Science
5. In **all art**

This order has a significant logic because, at first, there is a difference between science and art. Science **knows**, and art **creates**. To create (art) requires knowledge (science). To know you need wisdom. And wisdom comes from God, who gives it abundantly and without reproach (James 1:5). I used this verse that you taught me a long time ago, and even though I didn't remember where it was, I found it. I also learned with a Biblical Dictionary that Paul preached at the Ephesus theater (Acts). I talked about my experiences, and to end, he told them that **drama seasoned the Word**. He also said that theater was very **effective** because of its audiovisual platform. This means the person retains 50% of what it sees and 10% of what it hears. Therefore, theater guarantees that the person will retain 60%, and the Lord will take care of the other 40%. This indicates that for a non-believer, it is more effective than simple preaching, where he would only retain 10% of what he heard. Clarifying, of course, that he wasn't against it because the teaching was biblical but proving the effectiveness **of theater**.

Mayra used all that she learned in your classes given in Guaynabo for dramatization at churches. This is so you know that your words weren't gone with the wind; they were treasured, and today, we shared them with other churches.

Lizy

Note:

I met Lizy, as we affectionately called her, when I arrived at the Jardines de Caparra School. Lizette, along with her sister Mayra, were one of the first members of the Guariquén Theater Workshop, my first theater group. And then, I witnessed the redemptive work of Jesus in her life and in the life of her family.

Lizette became a news anchor and producer, being one of the most beautiful voices on Puerto Rican radio: "Radio loses a great voice and an incredible human being who for decades contributed to the media with responsibility and commitment to the country and the profession," said the Association of Journalists of Puerto Rico (ASPPRO) after Lizette's death.

Lizette is no longer with us but this letter that she sent me when I was a student in Bretton Hall College of the Arts, England, is one of my most precious treasures.

APPENDIX D
OPENING NEW PATHWAYS

Both Lizette Ayala's letter and this recognition are witnesses of a long journey. And although, in its beginnings, it seemed that the Word fell into a vacuum, today I realize that what Isaiah 55:11 tells us has been fulfilled:

> So shall My word be that goes forth from My mouth;
> it shall not return to Me void,
> but it shall accomplish that which I please,
> and it shall prosper in the thing for which I sent it.

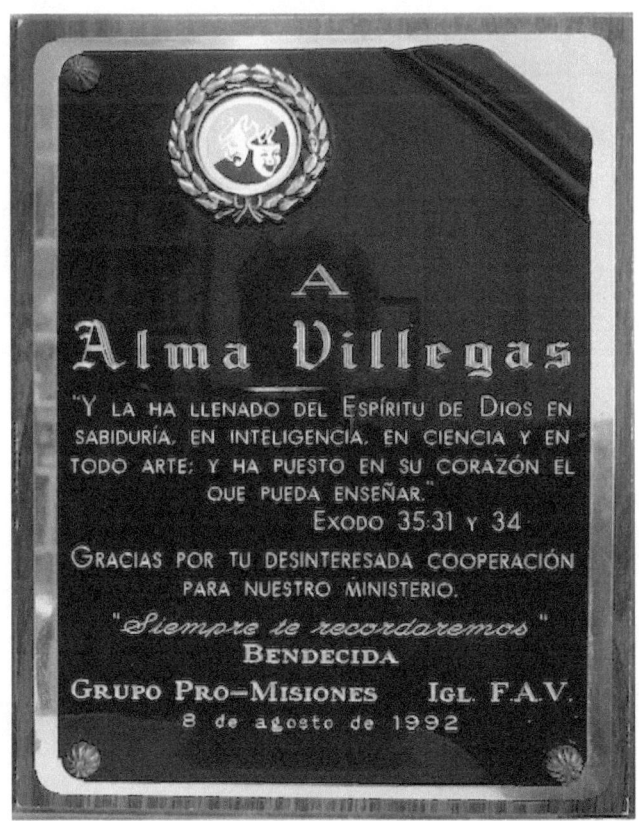

BIBLIOGRAPHY

Blue Letter Bible. *"Dictionary and Word Search."* Blue Letter Bible. 1996–2012.

Clarke, Adam. *Commentary on the Bible.* <http://www.sacred-texts.com/bib/cmt/clarke/exo.htm>.

Copeland, Kenneth. *The Kenneth Copeland Word of Faith Study Bible.* Modern English Version (MEV). Lake Mary, Florida: Published by Passio, 2017.

Dake, Finis Jennings. *Dake's Annotated Reference Bible.* Lawrence, Georgia: Dake Publishing, Inc., 2014.

Diccionario de la lengua española, © 2005 Espasa-Calpe, <http://www.wordreference.com/definicion/protocolo>.

Gordon, I., *Jesús en el Tabernáculo,* n.d.

Habershow, Ada R. *Outline Studies of the Tabernacle.* Grand Rapids, MI: Kregel Publications, 1974.

Hershberger, Ervin N. *Seeing Christ in the Tabernacle.* Harrisonburg, VA: Vision Publishers, 1995.

https://archive.org/details/ofplatobanquet00platrich/page/90/mode/2up.

https://biblestudentsdaily.com/2016/09/02/study-1-an-introduction-to-the-tabernacle-and-its-purpose/.

http://torah-art.net/index.php/portrait-artist-marty-shoub/.

https://www.biblegateway.com.

https://www.merriam-webster.com/dictionary.

Instituto Cultural Álef y Tau, A.C. *Biblia Peshitta en español.* Nashville: Broadmand & Holman Publishing Group, 2006.

Kalish, Edward Ephraim. *Bezalel, Son of Light*. Video.

Levi, David M. *The Tabernacle: Shadows of the Messiah*. Grand
    Rapids, MI: Kregel Publications, 2003.

Lledó, Emilio. *El concepto "poiesis" en la filosofía griega*. Madrid:
    Editorial DYKINSON, S.L., 2010.

Otto, Christ John. Bezalel, *Redeeming a Renegade Creation*. MA:
    Belonging House Creative, 2015.

Rand, W. W. *Diccionario de la Santa Biblia*. San Jose: Editorial
    Caribe, s.f.

Slemming, C. W. *Made According to Pattern*. Fort Washington, PA:
    CLC Publications, 1999.

Strong LL., S.T.D., James. *The New Strong's Expanded Exhaustive
    Concordance of the Bible*. Red Letter Edition. Nashville:
    Thomas Nelson, 2010.

Young, Robert. *Young's Analytical Concordance to the Bible*.
    Peabody, MA: Hendrickson Publishers, 2011

Vine, W.E. Edited by Merrill F. Unger, Th.M., Th.D., Ph.D. and
    William White, Jr., Th.M., Ph.D. *Vine's Complete Expository
    Dictionary of Old and New Testament Words*. Nashville:
    Thomas Nelson, 1996.

ABOUT THE AUTHOR
Alma Villegas, PhD, ThD

Author, Poet, Theater Director/Playwright/Independent Producer, Theater in Education Specialist, and Theology of Art Researcher

A LOOK AT THE IMPACT OF THE ARTS IN MY LIFE

My career began as a physics, biology, and chemistry teacher. However, during my first years as a teacher, I realized that the students were missing something that would season their lives. New paths had to be opened for them, and that something that they lacked, that way to open, was the way of art. Thus, with a group of high school students, I began my adventures in theater and the discovery of the impact that art can have on people's lives.

With this transformative vision, I returned to the University of Puerto Rico (UPR) to study theater. After finishing my studies at the UPR, I left for England, where I studied at Bretton Hall College of the Arts. In Bretton Hall, in addition to studying medieval theater and Shakespeare, I was able to study with several of the precursors of theater in education, such as actor and director John Hodgson. Upon my return from England, I continued studying at New York University (NYU), in the Department of Music and Performing Arts Professions, where I obtained a PhD in Educational Theater. And in August 2014, I received a doctorate in Christian Theology from the International Miracle Institute (IMI), Pensacola, FL.

GOD FULFILLS HIS PURPOSE IN US

I accepted Jesus as my Savior at the age of 16, at which time I started to attend the youth meetings at the *Iglesia Defensores de la Fe*, located on Comerio Street in Bayamón, with Rev. Leonardo Castro as pastor and Rafael Torres Ortega, Esq., as the youth pastor. I became an active member of the youth society. Together with a wonderful group of young people, I was one of the founding members of Grupo de Avivamiento, a choir that visited and continues to visit practically every town on the island of Puerto Rico, different countries throughout Latin America, and some US states with the message "Tiempo para cambiar" (Time to Change). Along with the Grupo de Avivamiento, I was able to visit the Dominican Republic, New York, New Jersey, Connecticut, Venezuela, Colombia, Guatemala, Mexico, and Chile.   I experienced thirteen years of spiritual growth and, at the same time, an intense evangelistic and missionary work.

As I grew in the Lord and developed my leadership within the youth, I also had the opportunity to attend the University of Puerto Rico (UPR) and obtain a Bachelor of Science with a major in agriculture and home economics.   These studies prepared me for and allowed me to work at isolated and/or special communities to minimize their physical, economic, and socio-cultural isolation. This would allow me to take my first steps towards the realization of a dream that had just started to be awakened: to combine art with missionary work in places where there was a great spiritual, economic, and socio-cultural need. I also attended the University of Bridgeport, where I received a master's degree in education with a concentration in biology.   After all of this, finally, I found the courage to go back to the University of Puerto Rico to study theater.

Throughout those formative years, I had the opportunity to preach, to be a Sunday school teacher, and to create for the local church the first Sunday school workshops for the children's teachers. However, it was in the area of art, more specifically in the area of theater, where my petition to God, "Lord make me a woman of ideas," started to be manifested within the Church as well as in the schools where I worked as a biology teacher. With the first ideas that I was developing and the incipient creative inspirations that I now understood were coming from God, I became, at a very early age, an independent theater producer and director, lighting, stage, and costume designer, actress, and playwright.   In those early days, I had no choice: if I wanted to do theater, I had to do it myself. It was a great school.

Even though, at Luis Pales Matos High School in Santa Rosa, Bayamon, I was a physics teacher, I decided, with a group of students, to create a journalism workshop, starting the newspaper

Clarín. This project, with the help of the school faculty, hosted the creation of the *Semana Palesiana* (Palesiano Week), responding to the students' lack of positive identity with the school. During that week, we painted murals, published a special newspaper issue commemorating the week, and filled the school with signs saying, "Estudiante Palesiano" (Palesiano Student). We also presented the Night of *Clarin*, a theater production that was written and directed by the student members of the journalism club; we invited well-known performing artists and civic and cultural leaders in Puerto Rico to come and give concerts and conferences to us. Among them, we had the presence of Jacobo Morales (actor, poet, and filmmaker) as a facilitator at a conference about Puerto Rican Culture and Sylvia del Villar (who offered an outstanding recital performance on the poetry of Luis Pales Matos). We hosted a literary contest and a program through WIPR Channel 6, a government-owned station, with Jesus Latimer, Dr. Margot Arce de Vazquez, and Ana Mercedes Pales (Luis Pales Matos's daughter). What impacted my life the most is that as of that first week of celebration, the theme "Estudiante Palesiano" (Palesiano Student) became part of the students' vocabulary, establishing a new episode in the life of the school that is still ongoing.

This experience exposed me to an unknown aspect of art, which, at the same time, brought a lot of questions. For the first time since my conversion, I was involved in secular work where art was the principal source, and the positive impact on the student body was highly visible. Would it be possible that God could use me as a positive-change instrument for something that many considered "worldly"? The answer was positive. And I witnessed how the arts were an agent of change in the student community.

Three years later, I became a teacher at Jardines de Caparra High School, another school in Bayamon. The small size of the school impacted me, as did the lack of artistic and cultural activities; there were practically none. It was then that I organized some theater workshops, and from them came the creation of Taller de Teatro Guariquén (Guariquén Theater Workshop). Guariquén is a Taino word meaning, "Look, come, and see." Tainos were the indigenous people of Puerto Rico. During the five years that I spent working with the theater group, I taught almost all aspects of theater arts, and I wrote, adapted, and developed around ten theater plays and screenplays for concerts that I was able to produce and direct.

This artistic work with the students was reflected throughout the community, which, in turn, started to experience the transforming power of art and its impact in society, bringing, as a consequence, to the members of the theater workshop all of their support. As an indirect result, many young people accepted Jesus as their personal Savior, and they were later followed by their parents. I emphasize "indirect result" because, as a teacher in the public education system, my goal was educational and cultural. And again, unexpected results were being manifested. What was moving those students to have an experience with God? I also witnessed how the arts were an agent of change, not only in the student community, but in the community at large. And here, I witnessed the second transformation, but this time, it went beyond the student community. This time, it reached the families of the students.

From the beginning of my development in the arts, I used theater, music, poetry, body movement, dance, pantomime, photography, biblical texts — especially the Psalms — as vehicles for education, personal development, and worship God. My artistic work, both carried out in the school and in the Church, was successfully presented throughout the island on television and in schools, hospitals, cultural centers, music conservatories, hotels, theaters, and churches. So, my pastor decided to give me a new challenge. By then, Rev. Rafael Torres Ortega was the senior pastor of the church. He allowed me to work next to him as an assistant producer of Encuentro (Encounter), an innovative Christian television program based on interviews with prominent Christian leaders and community leaders in general. My job was to design the introduction, select the music, and be the hostess for the guests before the beginning of the program, and sometimes I would be interviewed or become an interviewer if the guest didn't show up. This program was the basis for what later became one of the first Christian stations in Puerto Rico.

A CONVERSATION AND A CHALLENGE

One afternoon, as I was driving back home, God visited me in the car. I still remember the intensity of what I felt that day. The Lord spoke to my spirit about a calling. He told me that He was placing a different option before me than the one I had faced, that if I wanted to continue serving Him the same way, He would bless and prosper my way, but He was opening a new way before me. I understood in my spirit that the way would not be an easy one and that many years would pass by before I would see the manifestation of what God was speaking about. I had heard many times in church services through different preachings that God always has the best option. At that time, I started crying because I understood that my life was going to change dramatically, and I said, "Lord, I choose what you are offering me."

I always remember my last day at work on my way to study in England. As I was talking with one of the teachers, I looked at one of the blackboards, and God gave me a vision, and again I saw a long road, but since I was so committed and concentrated on my calling, I felt no fear nor intimidation about it. Besides, under the euphoria of the moment, I calculated that when the Lord spoke about many years, He was probably referring to five years. I am sure that the Lord smiled and felt at ease to know that I was not like the children of Issachar, experts in discerning the times. Maybe, if I had understood what God was speaking to me about, I would have remained in the comfort of my house and at the school where I was working. After all, I was serving the Lord and enjoying the positive results of my work.

Exodus 31 and 35, my conversations with God, the visions and prophetic words all confirmed the calling of God in my life; they reinforced my vocation towards theater, and they birthed the dream of continuing my advanced studies in theater and to study what the Bible said about art. I wanted to be ready for the arrival of the manifestation of my calling. I dreamed about teaching theater as the instrument of education, inspiration, healing, and transformation of communities around the world. I also dreamed of a supernatural manifestation of the spirit of creativity for the Church.

ART AS AN INSTRUMENT OF CHANGE

After the calling of God to my life, the doors to attend Bretton Hall College of the Arts in England and New York University in New York City opened widely. I left Puerto Rico to study and, at the same time, start a career in art that has brought me great satisfaction.

One of the most significant projects of my work in New York has been working in the prevention of HIV and the use of drugs within the Puerto Rican community. A program in creative arts was created and implemented to educate and empower the people who were affected by HIV/drugs throughout the community in general. Art was also used as an instrument of spiritual and emotional healing. As part of the strategy to work in the community, we opened a space called Manny Maldonado Theatre Gallery (1995–2005) to use it as a place of experimental and alternative theater. This was the first theater gallery that was opened in Williamsburg, Brooklyn, and it became a pioneering artistic movement of social transformation and of emotional and spiritual healing for a community that, until then, had been strongly whipped by drugs and HIV/AIDS.

As part of the work done at the theater gallery, we had 30 art exhibitions, 12 live theater performances, 10 outdoor festivals (concerts, theater, and dance), four indoor concerts, three spoken-word events, and a video festival. An art program was created for the community in general, including percussion and, on many occasions, piano, musical theory, dance, creative writing, and singing. We designed two public art exhibitions in two of the parks within the community, both dedicated to the AIDS epidemic; the United Nations documented one of them. A community that used to be identified primarily by its epidemic of drugs and AIDS, Williamsburg is today recognized in New York City and outside its limits as artistic and prosperous.

I understand that we were not the only ones in the transforming process of the community, but we played a leading role. Witnesses to this are the numerous awards, newspaper articles, radio interviews, and television programs that came to document the prevention work done through the arts, such as CNN in Spanish and Eyewitness News, ABC TV. Witnesses to this are also the presentations and demonstrations of the use of music in HIV prevention at national conferences, such as the Center for Disease Control and Prevention (CDC) in Atlanta, Georgia. And even more, participation in international conferences, such as the 12th World AIDS Conference in Geneva, Switzerland, and Women 2000: Women's Health Concerns in Latin America and the Caribbean in the 21st century, sponsored by the United Nations. And even an invitation to the White House, in Washington, D.C.

Thus, again, we witnessed another transformation. This time, the change was greater and more powerful because it reached an entire community and transformed drug addicts and people living with AIDS or HIV. God makes no distinction of person. He longs to reach all mankind.

In the area of theater production, the work done in the musical Civil War Voices by James R. Harris stands out. In it, I was part of the production team that won the Outstanding Production of a Musical Award at the 11th Midtown International Theater Festival (2010). The work won 11 nominations and six awards.

I was part of the Project CREO team, an Arts InterFACE initiative, which has developed an art project for children nationwide in Ecuador. During my stay in Quito, Ecuador, I gave seminars on acting, dramaturgy, and art theology. In addition, I directed an adaptation of the Song of Solomon, which I called *This is my Beloved*. It included body expression, music, and theater.

CONNECTING HEAVEN AND EARTH
THROUGH THEATRE

My mission in life is to make new paths and, in that journey along these new paths, transform people's lives and restore their creative spirit using the arts, especially the theater, as an instrument of inspiration, healing, and transformation.

I feel grateful to God because I understand that He gave me wisdom, knowledge, and, above all, the gift of art as an instrument to transform and literally save lives. The Bible tells us in Ephesians 3:20–21, "Now to Him who is able to do exceedingly abundantly beyond all that we ask or imagine, according to the power that works in us, to Him be the glory in the church and in Christ Jesus throughout all generations, forever and ever. Amen."

And I am a witness of such a creative abundance of God.

FOR MORE INFORMATION ABOUT

Theater Workshops and Theology of Art Seminars

www. TheGiftofArtInfo.com
www. AlmaVillegas.net

almavillegas@aol. com

Books

Bezalel Series

Bezalel, an Artist Called by God
Bezalel, an Artist Called by God: Study Guide and Creative & Artistic Activation

For those who prefer reading short books, I divided *Bezalel, an Artist Called by God* by its three main themes. It is also a good alternative for the young artist in your life.

God Chose an Artist: Bezalel's Call
Artist? God Has Six Gifts for You
Obedience and Submission, The Key to Bezalel's Success

Prophetic Performance Series

DECREES: Prophetic Performance
SIMBOLIC ACTIONS: Prophetic Performance
PROPHESIES, VISIONS & DREAMS: Prophetic Performance

Creative and Artistic Activation

The Creative Power of the Word of God for the Artist

Amazon.com

www.ingramcontent.com/pod-product-compliance
Lightning Source LLC
Chambersburg PA
CBHW021419210526
45463CB00001B/453